THE DARK FACE OF REALITY

Martin Israel was born in Johannesburg, where he qualified as a medical practitioner, subsequently migrating to Britain to further his medical education. In parallel with that he became increasingly involved in psychological and spiritual investigation, that culminated in his ordination to the Anglican priesthood in 1975.

He teaches pathology at the Royal College of Surgeons of England, and is also priest-in-charge of the church of Holy Trinity with All Saints in London. He is constantly engaged in the ministry of counselling and healing, and in conducting retreats all over the country.

Dr Israel has written a considerable number of books including *Summons to Life*, *Precarious Living*, *Smouldering Fire*, *The Pain That Heals*, *The Spirit of Counsel* (these published by Mowbrays), *Living Alone* (SPCK), *Healing as Sacrament* (Darton, Longman & Todd), *The Discipline of Love* (SPCK), *Coming in Glory* (Darton, Longman & Todd), *The Pearl of Great Price* (SPCK) and *Gethsemane* (Fount Paperbacks).

THE DARK FACE
OF REALITY

*A Study of
Emergent Awareness*

Martin Israel

Collins
FOUNT PAPERBACKS

First published in Great Britain by Fount Paperbacks,
London in 1989

Printed and bound in Great Britain by
William Collins Sons & Co. Ltd, Glasgow

To the memory of
James and Dorothy Parkes

How long, O Lord, have I cried to thee,
   unanswered?
I cry, "Violence!", but thou dost not save.
Why dost thou let me see such misery,
   why countenance wrongdoing?
Devastation and violence confront me;
   strife breaks out, discord raises its head,
   and so law grows effete;
   justice does not come forth victorious;
   for the wicked outwit the righteous,
   and so justice comes out perverted.

Habakkuk 1:1–4

The reckless will be unsure of himself,
   while the righteous man will live by his
   faithfulness.

Habakkuk 2:4

Contents

Prologue

The darkness of life has two distinct, though inter-weaving, strands. There is the darkness of personal suffering due to misfortune that we all have to undergo as part of our training to become useful citizens of the world. Without this testing experience we would be only too prone to complacency and selfishness. As we suffer, so we begin to enter into the pain of others, and the first step is made in understanding the meaning of corporate unity, that we are, in addition to being unique individuals in our own right, also parts of an immeasurably greater whole, the body of humanity, of creation itself.

But there is a more fundamental darkness that seems to be involved in, yet distinct from, this personal travail. It is a manifest power of evil that pervades the entire creative process and shows itself only too clearly in the cruelty people visit on each other and on the creation itself. A view of evil that sees it as only a privation of the good, though true enough in its own compass, seems to us, through the experience of our own lives, to be emphatically inadequate. There does appear to be a real, indeed assertive, force that is constantly conspiring to destroy all that is noble and good in the world. The enormities of our own century are too terrible to be attributed to mere ignorance, even if the power of evil does use human ignorance in its fell design of wreaking universal havoc. The passion of Christ is the paradigm of this cosmic drama, and it has been repeated on more than one occasion in the world's history since then – and no doubt before also.

We are moving to the close of a century torn apart with organized violence of such ferocity that those of us who have witnessed some of the drama of our time and are still alive, miraculously preserved in body and mind, quake inwardly at the sheer horror of it all. It is not unfitting that we should reflect on the phenomenon of evil, its part in cosmic destiny, and its ultimate healing. I use the word healing deliberately, because the cruder, if more satisfying, concept of destruction has been rendered increasingly inadequate by our greater understanding of the world. The advance of civilization adds to our knowledge of life on various levels: it is how we use the knowledge that determines the future of our civilization. In the past we could look back, for instance, on the isolated witness of the Jews, the Greeks, the Arabs, the Persians, the Indians and the Chinese, the history of all of whom had peaks of towering spiritual genius. But now we are a fully open world, and each group brings its gifts to enrich the whole. If even one of us is endangered, our fellows too are near the brink of destruction. We need a courageous integration of all mankind's long experience, good and bad alike, for the work ahead of us. It is a sobering, but also invigorating, reflection that God is the creator of all things, whether seen or unseen, and that what he has made is fundamentally good, no matter what changes it may have to undergo in the course of its strange unfolding, its tortured, slow, yet magnificent development, to adult stature and service. In the agony of pain beyond articulate communication. . . we are sustained by a hope so precious that all past suffering seems entirely logical, even worthwhile, for we have glimpsed the divine reality. But it is we who then have to make the journey, like Abraham, from the world of the senses to the Promised Land. In the end the two come together in the love of God.

1

The Faces of Darkness and Light

As the night comprises the other half of the daylight, so does darkness complement the light of human sight. Its shadow lies in the heart of each of us as we set about our livelihood precariously in the light of the day. It reminds us how close we all are to the primordial chaos out of which creation evolved. And so, not far beneath the smiling face of our present ease, there lies an ominous dark presence. It never ceases to draw the mind back to the unpleasant episodes of the past, on which the present moment has its foundation, as it casts a threatening shadow on the plans ahead of us. How little control do we indeed have over the course of even a small part of our life; how much are we at the mercy of unpredictable cosmic forces, to say nothing of the emotions that dominate our actions! The vast range of the unconscious is occupied by a darkness inhabited by various emotional elements that can wreak terrible havoc on our lives, but yet have in them the propensity for creative imagination if properly harnessed. The seething dark forces of destruction boil inwardly like the lava of a simmering volcano, apt to erupt at any time, able both to destroy the life around it and to pour down into the wider plain beneath, thus increasing its lethal potential.

It is little wonder that the reflective type of person learns to count his blessings day by day, and if of a superstitious frame of mind, to placate and ingratiate the intelligence that governs his little world. In this way he hopes that the time of good fortune may be prolonged, and that subterranean disorder may stay away from his abode. And yet there is a larger, more adult awareness of the inevitability of destruction and chaos, of a darkness close even to the transitory experience of bliss. We hang on to youth, to success, to happiness, while we know with inescapable certainty that all is founded on a seething tide of change, enfeeblement and death. Did not the prosperous Job sacrifice unfailingly to God after his rather empty-headed children had celebrated together, lest in their unreflecting levity, perhaps roused up by drink, they might have blasphemed the Name of God? Did not the boy Jesus know, even as he sat entranced at the learning and disputations of the doctors of the Law in the temple at Jerusalem, that he had to be continually about his Father's business? And this business was not only the light of teaching and healing, but also the darkness of jealousy, passion and death. At the same time his distracted parents suffered agony as they believed he was lost on the way home; the joy of his presence was overlaid by the pain of his absence on a mission far beyond their understanding. The hour that shows us the light of day prepares us for the time of darkness which no man can avoid. It may be the comforting darkness that envelops us as we move wearily towards rest and sleep, but in due course it assumes more threatening undertones as life moves towards its end: impersonal oblivion, incapacity and final death. In the darkness of the night much is revealed of our inner life from which we would flinch during the diverting work of the hours of coming day. Activity of a worldly type forms a protective barrier against contact with inner truths of loneliness and panic, but there comes a time when nothing can remain hidden as we assume the full stature of a human being. And so the light of day may conceal what the darkness of the night brings into exquisite focus. In the light of human conviviality we may act with conviction a stereotyped role according to wonted tradition, but in the black solitude the role is personal and authentic. In the end the darkness has to inform the light no less than the light to illuminate the darkness. Each has valuable teaching to bestow so that a life beyond the dualities may emerge. This is the life of integrity. It is the life of God beyond the dualities of darkness and light, in which the uncreated light embraces and transfigures both earthly light and subterranean darkness.

In early life we seem to be balanced precariously on a pinnacle of radiant promise that is subtly and persistently undermined by disorder of cosmic proportions, yet concentrated into the little world of fellow creatures among whom we live and work. The disorder gnaws at the foundation of our apparent stability, which is the life of common endeavour in which we pass each moment in personal aspiration lit by the glow of suffused hope. In the biblical story this undermining power is in perpetual conflict with all that leads the human to the vision of God. It seeks to sully all that is noble and beautiful in our lives. It makes its appearance in the creation allegory, when the serpent, the most crafty of God's creatures, seduces Eve – and then her husband Adam – away from the path of obedience to the will of God. They then are expelled from the sanctuary of heaven and fall into the limited sphere of mortal life. The darkness of death awaits them patiently yet hungrily as mortal life drains from them. There is no magic path back to what was lost through ignorance and self-seeking, but instead the way is shown of an onerous, onward journey of increasing self-knowledge in the pitiless wastes of matter, coarse and uncomprehending. Indeed, it seems to be the function of the human race to infuse that coarseness and illuminate that incomprehension with so great a love that all living forms may finally be freed from the prison of death and enter upon a travelled path leading to enlightenment and final resurrection. But first the coarseness of matter must be appreciated and the imprisonment of darkness experienced. The fear we all know in closed space and undefined darkness can be dispelled only by the presence of the Living God, a presence that must be known before an advance into the silent stretches of darkness can be tolerated without the advent of terror, if not sheer panic. This may be our clue to a mature understanding of heaven, an atmosphere (or realm, or dimension depending on the metaphor preferred) inhabited by diverse creatures working in trustful collaboration, instead of merely the single unaware couple, Adam and Eve, ungrateful for and oblivious of the bliss that encompassed them. And so, while death cuts short the plight of Adam and Eve, irrevocably shut out of the heaven of intimate communion with their Father and all their fellow creatures, there remains the hope of a resurrection to new heights of spiritual stature into that full proper man whose name is Jesus in the Christian revelation. Other faiths will proclaim their own particular master, but the acid test of validity is the effect that individual has had in lightening the burden of humanity and illuminating the darkness of the cruel, unresponsive world of matter.

Where there is heaven there is no darkness, for everything lies revealed, open to the gaze of everyone and radiating a love that holds all in its blessing. And so St John can say in his first letter (1:5) that God is wholly light without a trace of darkness. Where there is darkness, a shadow falls upon the person who may, like Adam and Eve, use it to hide from the gaze of their fellow creatures, even the very presence of God. But the shadow does not conceal anything to those outside it. Only those who cast it believe it can shield them from the consequences of their actions. To those who can see, or more pertinently have had their sight restored – like the man born blind whom Jesus healed, well described in the ninth chapter of the Fourth Gospel – little remains hidden even when enveloped in a dense cloud. The basis of this penetrating vision is the divine essence pouring from those whom God has healed, so that they are endued with an intensity of spiritual sight that can penetrate the deepest mysteries of creation. This is, in fact, a measure of a person's spiritual proficiency: he can look into himself unflinchingly as through plain glass, and by his own searing self-knowledge see into the hearts of his fellow creatures with a similar clarity. However, the energy that directs spiritual vision is love, and in its glow there is no judgement but only an all-embracing acceptance of all that exists. And then the truth can be known, and its burden gradually assimilated by those who seek the way of God even to their own suffering.

If the Fall heralds man's departure from the heavenly state in the Old Testament, the tragic story of Ananias and Sapphira in the fifth chapter of the Acts of the Apostles outlines it in the New Dispensation. In the early apostolic period, the disciples were so filled with the Holy Spirit that had been fully released within them after they had acknowledged the Lordship of Christ that they had no need of material possessions to substantiate their sense of fulfilment. And so all they possessed was held in common; their identity in this new heaven depended on their membership of the body of believers, and did not require individual gifts or talents to confirm it: each contributed his own particular gift to the whole community, which in turn provided its support. In its limits he could attain his own spiritual development. And so the Cypriot Levite Joseph, surnamed Barnabas (which means "Son of Exhortation"), sold a large estate and laid the proceeds at the apostles' feet. By contrast, Ananias and his wife Sapphira held back some of the purchase money on a property they sold, and pretended that the sum they gave the apostles was the full amount. The darkness of cupidity had cast its shadow on the very portals of heavenly accord, and the erring couple found themselves inextricably bound to that shadow. They had, through their dishonesty, shut out the Holy Spirit from their lives, and so, once confronted by Peter with their sin of lying to God's Spirit, they dropped down dead. This is a dramatic example of the sin against the Holy Spirit for which death in one form or another is an inevitable consequence, inasmuch as the Spirit of

God is the giver of life, without whom a living creature falls back into a lifeless corpse of inert matter. We may look in inspired hope for the later forgiveness and restoration of this sadly misguided couple – and the multitudes who have subsequently followed the same path of perjury in the pursuance of covetousness – once they have confessed their sin, but their immediate fate is pitiable: falling into the opaque featurelessness of death, isolated and friendless. So it is with all who withdraw into the caves of darkness to commit sins against humanity, which is tantamount to blaspheming the Name of God and undermining all he has set up. It becomes increasingly apparent that the advent of darkness follows the creature's transgression, showing itself when he excludes himself from the light. And yet all is embraced within the creative fiat of God, and matter never ceases to be holy.

It is an ironic variation of this theme of darkness and light that possessions cast their shadow, while in a state of blessed poverty all is bright. The more one has, the more one desires, and greed soon trespasses the bounds of the law to assuage its ravenous appetite. And so the wealthy tend to move uneasily in the borderland of lawful profit and subtle crime. The greater the riches, the greater the darkness. One can almost, but not quite, envy the hero of George Gershwin's opera *Porgy and Bess* who sings

> I got plenty of nuttin'
> and nuttin's plenty for me.

On a more scriptural note, the first Beatitude blesses the poor in spirit, those who know their need of God – for they already have the Kingdom of Heaven, hence they are in fellowship with the Most High, and all lesser considerations fall into their proper place. Possessions and attitudes of mind are transfigured in the light of God's love, and become ways of serving the greater community of life. As Jesus teaches later in the Sermon on the Mount, "Set your mind on God's Kingdom and his justice before everything else, and all the rest will come to you as well" (Matthew 6:33). Porgy, in the direct, unsophisticated manner of the truly lowly person – who is also a natural discerner of spirits – knew this by intuition, and so everything he touched took on a spiritual radiance. This applied even to the woman he loved, on the surface a feeble chattel of men's lust, but at heart also a child of God, weak as flesh but yearning for the acceptance born of love.

We come, in the great vision of Wordsworth's *Ode to the Intimations of Immortality*, trailing clouds of glory from God who is our home. As we incarnate more and more completely in the world of grit, dirt and slime, so the darkness forms a dense encrustation around our personality, an accretion of compliant conformity in a world of blind covetousness. Shielded by and concealed within that crust we can participate in the underhand intrigues that characterize mundane existence, with its sordid goal of material success, if need be to the exclusion of any nobler vision. And yet the crust that shuts out the light is as much a part of our worldly condition as is the radiance of God's love. It is fortunate that monotheistic religion sees all things in the creative control of God, all under his aegis. And so the realm of darkness we have inherited as part of our collective responsibility as members of the human race is one we are destined to explore. We cast its shadow on the fair earth beneath us, but even when it clouds our spiritual as well as our rational vision, it too is permeated by the uncreated light of God who is the master of eternity. The opacity of matter is our first definitive experience of darkness, for it is inert, largely unresponsive and unreflective by its very nature. On it, in it, and through it we, creatures both of material opacity and spiritual light, work out our destiny, and in this essentially self-centred act we can either destroy or create. If we work in the service of the light, that light issues from us to illuminate the hidden, the unexplored regions of the earth. But if the work is self-centred and crassly insensitive to the needs of others, the innocence at the heart of nature is desecrated, and darkness covers the trail we have set up. In the words of the prologue to the Fourth Gospel, the light shines on in the dark, and the darkness has never mastered it. But we can say with equal assurance, born of bitter experience, that the light will never master the darkness of the universe until it has so inflamed the souls of all God's creatures that they become participants in a universal transfiguration that will herald the coming in glory of the One Who Is. In him alone is the light's mastery unchallenged, because it flows out in loving radiance, not a brilliant glare that blinds rather than enlightens. And so all is accepted in love and presented to the Father for final resurrection.

It should be emphasized, lest one is tempted to fall into a heretical gnosticism that sees matter as fundamentally evil and the earth a place of imprisonment from which to escape at all costs, that everything that God has created – and creation never stops, for it continues until the time of final consummation – is good. This theme occupies the first chapter of the Book of Genesis. As the creation story unfolds to the tragedy of the Fall, so the fundamental light of the world darkens, and its radiant energy slows down to a less responsive solidity. The creature has started to exert his baneful effect on the environment, just as man's departure from God heralds bitter internecine strife, evidenced tragically in the murder of Abel by Cain, and his progressive desecration of the earth. This precedes the story of the Flood, in the course of which God destroys everything except the just man Noah and his family (and samples of all living animals). When the waters recede and the ark touches solid earth, a new covenant is proclaimed: the human may henceforth feed on animals (provided they are drained of blood, the traditional life-force of the creature) in contradistinction to the older covenant when both the human and the animal fed exclusively on plant life. And so the era of callous animal exploitation, with its attendant cruelty, is inaugurated.

Of course, no one except the literalist (a more satisfactory term than fundamentalist, which can at least theoretically have a number of different nuances) would accept all this as a historical account of the early years of the world, but the underlying spiritual truth is evident to anyone with imagination and experience of human nature. St Paul expands on this theme in the glorious eighth chapter of his letter to the Romans:

For the whole created universe waits with eager expectation for God's sons to be revealed. It was made the victim of frustration, not by its own choice but because of him who made it so; yet always there was hope, because the universe itself is to be freed from the shackles of mortality and enter upon the liberty and splendour of the children of God. Up to the present we know the whole created universe groans in all its parts as if in the pangs of childbirth. Not only so, but even we, to whom the Spirit is given as firstfruits of the harvest to come, are groaning inwardly while we wait for God to make us his sons and set our whole body free. For we have been saved, though only in hope (8:19–24).

It is indeed the bringing into full manifestation of this hope that is the way of lightening the world's darkness and overcoming the sting of mortality. Matter, however, as indeed all that God has created, retains an essence of goodness despite the tragedy – in my view inevitable – of the Fall. If God did not actively plan it, he certainly had contingency plans available for its eventuality. By the nature of free will selfish actions are inevitable as part of the individual's growth, and these cloud the transparency of the created order as the protagonists huddle together in the darkness they have created in order to plan further destructive action under the ironic guise of self-advancement. And yet it is the darkness rather than the light that is the most fertile medium of growth. We can once again, in company with the writer of Psalm 139, celebrate God's over-all supremacy, that he is the master alike of heaven and hell, of the light and the darkness. But in our mundane existence he seems all too often to have surrendered his control to less exalted agents, and here lies the tragedy as well as the glory of the human situation.

What is indeed this light that St John identifies with God, and whose is the darkness that has no place in him? Certainly the bitter experience of pain and suffering can open up the gaze of even untutored people to a reality far wider than anything that may be read of in texts or taught by well-schooled phil-osophers and theologians. Did not the young unknown Jesus of Nazareth speak to the masses with an authority completely lacking in the recognized teachers of the Law? He apparently had had no known rabbinic training, indeed his very antecedents were so plebeian that none could associate his under-standing with his background. God the Son he was indeed, but he, as an emptied human being, had to know and actualize his godhead through the mani-fold experiences of his everyday life. And then he could know the Father so intimately that he was in complete union with him, even when the darkness of hell obliterated any visible trace of that relation-ship. He knew God in the light of day, groped after him in the darkness of passion, and came completely into his presence when death had claimed a victory over the mortal man. Somehow we too are called upon to tread this path, to experience the sequence, so that divine wisdom may illuminate and transfigure the worldly knowledge we have attained in the shadow region of reality. The path to heaven must inevitably traverse long stretches of hell, for every part of the drab landscape has to be known, accepted and loved. God is never far from any creature, but it is we who have to draw out the divine essence at the heart of reality.

2

The Human Situation

We read in Ecclesiasticus 15:11–15:

> Do not say, "The Lord is to blame for my failure";
> it is for you to avoid doing what he hates. Do not
> say, "It is he who has led me astray"; he has no
> use for sinful men. The Lord hates every kind of
> vice; you cannot do it and still fear him. When he
> made man in the beginning, he left him to take his
> own decision; if you choose, you can keep the
> commandments; whether or not you keep faith is
> yours to decide.

He goes on, in the manner of Deuteronomy 30:15-
20, to remind us that God has set before us fire and
water, and it is we who have to choose; before man
lie life and death, and whatever he prefers is his. But
above this free choice God sees everything and
watches over those who fear him. In the letter of St
James which is, to a certain extent, a New Testament
follow-up of Ecclesiasticus, we are reminded once
more that God does not tempt us, for he is untouched
by evil and does not himself tempt anyone. He goes
on to observe that temptation comes when a man is
enticed and lured away by his own lust; the lust
conceives, and give birth to sin; and sin full-grown

breeds death (1:13–15). Certainly it may be true that God does not directly tempt us, but he does seem to allow the dark forces to attack us, perhaps to test and build up our spiritual capacity – the story of Satan's attack on Job's welfare is a classical development of this theme.

So the Bible certainly affirms our God-given free will, but also points to the tragic weakness in character we all, to a greater or lesser extent, seem to inherit. Contemporary schools of social and psycho-dynamic thought tend to dismiss any idea of effective free will, so enslaved, so they would have us believe, is the human to vast, impersonal economic forces on the one hand and to psychological conditioning, both personal and communal, on the other. That the human has an inborn capacity to sin is inferred in Psalm 51:5, "In iniquity I was brought to birth and my mother conceived me in sin". St Paul develops this theme of "original sin" in Romans 5:12–21, demonstrating how the primal sin of Adam, inherited by all subsequent generations, has been annulled by the sacrificial death of Jesus, which has initiated a new dispensation. Nevertheless, we are bound to acknowledge, in all due realism, that the full manifestation of this new dispensation is still far away: in the words of Paul already quoted, "We have been saved, though only in hope" (Romans 8:24). The great act of salvation may have already taken place on a cosmic plane, as Paul indicates in the letters to the Colossians and Ephesians – if indeed the latter is a completely Pauline work – but it may also be that this act will be made manifest in our world only with the Second Coming. All the great religions eagerly await this, even if they each use a different name for the universal saviour whom the Christian sees in Jesus.

It is interesting to follow up this speculation with Paul's views in the ninth chapter of his letter to the Romans. It broaches the vexing question of personal responsibility for sin in the face of divine omnipotence, but can only go so far as to assert God's power of free choice in deciding whom he accepts and whom he rejects – the election of Jacob over his older twin Esau is a case in point, as is also the story of Cain and Abel. But why was Esau intellectually and spiritually inferior to Jacob, and why was Cain of violent temperament as compared with the poignant innocence of his brother Abel? St Paul can offer no rational answer to this dilemma of apparently arbitrary predestination; he simply says we are not entitled to interrogate God, in the same way as the pot cannot hold the potter to account if it is misshapen. One cannot deny the disappointment one feels at this summary closure of the debate just when the argument was becoming really interesting, even if Paul does soften matters by stressing the divine patience and mercy: God tolerates the vessels which are objects of retribution due for destruction in order to make known the full wealth of his splendour upon vessels which were objects of mercy, and which from the first had been prepared for this splendour (vv. 23–24). When he translates this analogy to the young Christian community, the vessels due for divine splendour are the congregation of Jewish and Gentile converts, whereas the majority of Jews who refuse to accept Jesus as Christ are rejected and relegated to a back position until the event of their conversion, which, as he writes later with great sadness tinged with delicate hope, is unlikely to take place for a long time. "But if their offence means the enrichment of the world, and if their falling-off means the enrichment of the Gentiles, how much more their coming to full strength!" (Romans 11:12). One might add, with the touch of irony born of twenty centuries of Christian witness, that most practising Christians through the ages were quite as far from the spirit of their Saviour as were the Jews who continued to deny his sovereignty. Fortunately this sad travesty of true Christianity has been constantly redeemed by the witness of the few saints present in every generation of Christians – and of Jews also, for Christ far transcends parties and denominations.

And so we have the paradox of God's gift of free will dispersed among a population who are largely incapable of using it effectively. Like the hundred and twenty thousand of Jonah's Nineveh, they cannot tell their right hand from their left. Like the crowds at the Crucifixion event, they look on in malicious curiosity, while Jesus calls on his Father to forgive them, for they do not know what they are doing. They are so unformed as individuals that they can be led astray by any vociferous demagogue who plays on their baser emotions or any event that does not fulfil their expectations. One does indeed wonder whether free will is an illusion until one remembers the many quiet, decent members of society who go about their business with honesty and charity, despite the temptation to take a devious short-cut to prosperity. Their crown is the glorious company of saints already referred to, but in its wider context the word should include the members of a worshipping community, all going about their own business for the

greater good of the whole. This should extend ultimately to mankind in general as well as the person's
local group. There is, in other words, a wide spec-
trum of humanity, ranging from the many who seem
barely to have graduated from their animal ancestry
to a progressively smaller number who have
explored the spiritual world and are the pioneers of a
new style of life, one that is no longer carnally
orientated but has learnt to discipline the flesh for the
benefit of the wider community. When we consider
the starving millions who inhabit many of the undeveloped countries of the world, it seems evident that
a vast human population has no effective hope at all
of any mental, let alone spiritual, growth in this life.
But even in this mass of degraded humanity there is
not infrequently a dignified spirituality that may
indeed be nearer the truth than the worldly-wise
agnosticism of many of the prosperous members of
the affluent western nations. We judge by appearances, but God looks into the heart, as Samuel was
told in the matter of the anointing of the shepherd
David. In the work of counselling and the ministry
of healing one never ceases to be amazed at the
courage and faith of people who have come from the
most terrible backgrounds and have won through by
sheer faith and hard work. On the other hand, not a
few of the opulent members of the developed countries are slaves to drugs, drink, sex or the occult
scene, that effectively preclude any intellectual or
spiritual development to full personality. Only when
they have asserted their free will, clouded but never
defunct, to resist the temptation to this terrible
thraldom, can there be genuine spiritual growth.

But can an addicted or indoctrinated person muster

the inner strength to make this final break with old ways of thought, to renounce evil and start the movement back to sanity, health and God? There can be glib affirmations about the power of Christ, but this power cannot act until the person is prepared to play his part. The contest between Augustine and Pelagius – concerning the relative efficacy of divine grace and the human will to change – may have been decided officially in favour of St Augustine's insistence on the powerlessness of man and his absolute dependence on God's grace, but in fact there has also to be an initial receptivity of the person to God's grace. This is the essence of human free will. In other words, we can either accept the love of God or else reject it, whether through indifference, pride or malice. And until we repent of our hardheartedness we stay as we are. God himself, whose nature is love, cannot force himself on us without abrogating the kind of relationship he has ordained, one that has been in action since the time of creation. God is courteous, as Julian of Norwich was shown in her *Revelations of Divine Love*: he respects the privacy of the beloved and does not force himself on any of his rational creatures, whom he has endowed with freedom of choice. This is the full measure of love: to grant freedom to the beloved to go his own way, even when it is obvious that only disaster lies ahead of him, but to remember him constantly in prayer and to be ready to receive him back home again without recrimination when he comes to himself and repents of his folly. And then the beloved, typified by the Prodigal Son in the famous parable, is amazed at the warmth that enfolds him. Such love is divine in power, and it initiates a new relationship between

the person and God and also between him and his
fellow creatures. Love knows no judgement; this it
leaves to the beloved when he returns to his right
frame of mind. In the end even the most terrible
human condemnation falls away in the face of human
love, which, in turn, is but a pale reflection of divine
love. We love because God loved us first (1 John
4:19).

It is evident that only the few are fully responsive
to God's love; they are humble and open to the
unceasing wonder of life, which is taken for granted
by most of us in bored ingratitude. "How blest are
those whose hearts are pure; they shall see God"
(Matthew 5:8). On the whole, children are more
open to the divine presence because their minds are
innocent, free of preconceptions and therefore
unclouded in perception. Theirs is a world of simplicity, for their wants are elementary and easily
satisfied by those who care for them. True simplicity
has a purity that is absolutely necessary for the vision
of God. But nevertheless it is our common lot to
enter the shuddering maelstrom of adult working life
before that purity can be convincingly tested. It is
one thing to be a delightful child around whom one's
little world revolves, but quite another to retain that
simplicity of life style and purity of heart in the daily
struggle of competitive existence. It is hard not to
fall into sin, which is seen most practically as the
tendency to exalt one's own needs and desires above
those of other people, to their ultimate detriment.
The end of this tendency is a progressive depreciation
of all those outside the sinner's intimate circle –
which finally narrows down to one person only, and
he is left with neither human friend nor divine

intimacy. The wage of sin is indeed death (Romans 6:23), for it progressively shuts one off from the life-giving power of the Holy Spirit. And so one slides imperceptibly into a darkness peopled by regrets rather than human company. But death itself can be the harbinger of a new life, as the Prodigal Son was to discover; by comparison, his formally correct brother was as far from that life at his return as when the young man had left home and wasted all his resources in the irresponsible behaviour that was to end in the death of his old self. From this example we can begin to see the way of growth from the bored unawareness of the man in the street to the intimate relationship with God which I believe we are all meant to share. And so darkness can bring us closer to the divine light than the glitter of material success coveted by the unaware multitudes.

But let us beware of sneering at material success – this is done most effectively by people who have failed to attain it, whether professionally or financially! To do well in life is preferable to the reproach of never having made a go of anything. The ultimate spiritual value of material success is, paradoxically, the experience of renunciation that is entailed as the person retires from work and gradually fades into darkening oblivion; his body becomes decrepit, as does apparently his reputation also, for new lights appear in the worldly firmament that seem to out-shine anything he may have achieved in his own day. By contrast, the life of one who has continually failed to achieve anything proceeds, and is snuffed out, not so much with a bang as a whimper, as T. S. Eliot expresses it so movingly at the end of *The Hollow Men*. But there is hope also for the unsuccessful person, provided he does his best in the face of discouragement, refuses to lapse into bitterness, blaming other people or circumstances for his failures, and counts his many blessings in the face of the tragedies of the world around him, which in our era of mass communication includes the wretched of the whole earth. The same approach applies to those who are so physically or mentally ill that there seems to be no future for them in the world of affairs. Whereas chronic disease of the body evokes immediate sympathetic concern, mental trouble usually tends to repel most bystanders, since the victim often does not communicate in an acceptable way and arouses irritation rather than compassion. But to have come through a mental illness is a great achievement, for now one can communicate with a large range of people in a way that the normal, unafflicted individual could not even begin to fathom. This is in fact merely a variation of the theme of the enlightened Prodigal Son who has learnt to receive, and therefore to give, love, while the inexperienced brother remains cold and aloof.

We are left with the conundrum of human beings endued with free will and almost certain to take the wrong turning. The Prodigal Son did come to himself in destitution, but many more never seem to arrive. The sacred history of the Jews as recorded in the Old Testament is a heartrending illustration of this theme. From the time of the exodus from Egypt to the Babylonian exile about six hundred and fifty years later, there is the recurrent event of apostasy, defeat, suffering, prayer to God for forgiveness, the appearance of a new champion (whether judge, king or prophet), victory, relaxation and further apostasy.

The prophets exhort the people to righteousness, but they respond too little and too late. The ministry of Jeremiah is the outstanding illustration of this trend. He started his work during the closing years of Josiah, one of the three beneficial kings of Judah (David and Hezekiah were the other two), and continued during the reign of disastrously wicked rulers who led the people increasingly astray. The first part of Jeremiah's prophecy is one of threats of national disaster if the people do not repent; however, there comes the watershed after which national destruction by the Babylonians is inevitable, and the prophet urges the rulers to capitulate before the Holy City and its temple are razed to the ground. Of course, such a prophecy immediately tars Jeremiah with the brush of a traitor, and he suffers accordingly. In the end his prophecy is fulfilled almost to the letter. In the account we see the relative balance of free will and predestination. Since the will of the people and the later kings was paralysed, ruin was inevitable. However, had Jeremiah's prophecy been heeded early on, events might have taken a different course. The story of Jonah and the conversion of the people of Nineveh indicates the possibility of a change in events even at a late hour, provided there is genuine repentance and a firm will to amend the national life style. Alas, the Book of Jonah is merely inspired fiction, whereas that of Jeremiah is historical! Admittedly the prophet Micah, who lived a century before Jeremiah, had shocked the inhabitants of Jerusalem with a similar type of prophecy, and they were saved from the destructive Assyrian army, but their will to change was, as usual, short-lived, and they soon lapsed into idolatry again.

And so we read the despairing rhetorical question of Jeremiah 13:23, "Can the Nubian change his skin or the leopard his spots?" The passage goes on to ask whether the people of Israel can do good, they who are schooled in evil. This fearful passage ends with terrible threats of punishment for the adulterous people, some of which had already taken place. It is a perennial problem of human nature, whether we can change ourselves to any significant extent. In the question posed above, the answer is clearly in the negative. Christ himself teaches that the most anxious thought cannot add a foot to one's height (Matthew 6:27). It is evident that our basic temperament is innate, and we have to make the most of it. But our character, seen in terms of moral strength and spiritual aspiration, is something that we develop with the passage of years. The artistic temperament, for instance, may be associated with gross moral irresponsibility or it may be the basis of inspiration to the whole world. Our personality is integrated as we learn to recognize, accept and use the various gifts, defects and accomplishments with which we have been endowed, and at the end of our mortal life we, like the crucified Christ, may say, "It is accomplished", and "Father, into thy hands I commit my spirit". It is important to see even our defects in this creative light: once again the returned Prodigal Son is our paradigm.

But all this pertains to essentially healthy people. What are we to say about those who are born so mentally defective that a normal working life is denied them? On the other side of the coin there is the tragic deterioration in mental function that attends progressive brain disease, especially in the elderly. To see a formerly esteemed member of the community, with a vivid appreciation of life, gradually sinking into a vegetable state of torpor, scarcely able to react to any outside stimulus, and certainly unresponsive to the love of those closest to him, is a tragedy beyond description. What has happened to the personality? Indeed, who is the person sitting inertly before us? Are we, after all, merely bodily machines controlled by a master organ, the brain, and driven passively by any circumstance that impinges upon our basic needs of survival, procreation and comfort? It is certain that various authorities have their own views about the mind-brain relationship and the possible survival of the personality beyond bodily death, but no statement is more than an individual opinion, and in the end we lesser mortals have to fashion our own system of belief based on our personal experiences and modified by the findings of contemporary science. The freedom to acknowledge this agnosticism is an enormous relief, for now we are able to make our own journeys and be open to what life is telling us as we proceed a day at a time. The various religious systems have come into being as the result of spiritual geniuses formulating their insights into a coherent philosophy that can guide their fellows into a more satisfactory way of life and help them to develop into more fully actualized individuals. But none has the complete truth; this pertains to God alone, in whom only can our questions find an answer. In this life the answer can be only tentative because so much of the background of personal experience remains hidden.

The experience of a higher power comes unheralded, often when we least expect it and frequently when we are at a particularly low ebb. Suddenly a light appears in our mental horizon and we can, in a flash, see what was previously incomprehensible. It fills us with hope sufficient to continue the long trail, and as we proceed, more is revealed so that life itself takes on a new radiance. But is this experience an illusion, a mere will-o'-the-wisp that peters out as it leads us astray? We can never be certain, but one thing is clear: it has altered the tenor of our life so that relationships with others become easier and our own creativeness is enhanced. The ultimate criterion is that of Jesus, "You will recognize them by the fruits they bear" (Matthew 7:16). It is in the spirit of this guidance that faith is monitored by common sense, and the will to proceed forwards drives us relentlessly on the path of life. The harvest of the divine spirit in human life is specified in Galatians 5:22: love, joy, peace, patience, kindness, goodness, fidelity, gentleness and self-control. Even a slight movement in their direction must be the right one. This is the basis of a living faith in the face of the darkness that so often encompasses us in the cut and thrust of mortal existence.

And so perhaps we may come to some slight resolution of the problem of human free will and divine predestination. If God is love and he cherishes everything he has made, it seems not unreasonable to believe that the destiny he wills for all his creatures is development, transfiguration and eternal life in his glory. The apparent hopelessness of the present situation, the evil that surrounds us, and the pain we all have to bear during this transient life on earth, are part of a much greater vision of reality. But we, as the rational creatures of our little world, are given the immense privilege of working with God to the fulfilment of his will. If we fall into sin, we regress to the process of decay that typifies the creation in its naked form; if we live a life of love made manifest in service to others, we begin to move beyond the destruction in store for all living things, and play our part in redeeming these also from the prison of death. The theme of the eighth chapter of Paul's letter to the Romans amplifies this, as we have already noted. Therefore the more animal-like our style of living, the more we follow the animals to the dust of the earth, which is our common mortal destiny. But as we move to a truly human aspiration, so we begin to play our part in the healing of the world, and our own end comes to show something of the glory of the crucified Christ. To be sure, our mortal bodies, unlike that of Jesus, are destined for the common grave of the earth's soil, in company with all our animal brethren, but something of our presence continues in a life beyond common death, where perhaps we may continue our work of loving service to the glory of God, the end being the resurrection of the whole world. But this far-off event to which the whole creation moves is beyond our simple comprehension, and the wise person keeps his counsel in awe and reverence.

The older one gets, the more evident does it become how the general pattern of one's life has been pre-ordained. Indeed, we are all so much parts of the body of mankind that we seem to have been specially endowed with a unique personality with which to serve the whole. But what really matters in the final reckoning is whether we have played our part well, or have, like the stupid servant in the Parable of the

Talents (Matthew 25:14–30), wasted our time by burying our gift in a life of selfish indulgence on the one hand or simple apathy and inaction born of unawareness on the other. As we grow into authentic people, so we can, by our enlightened will, make our contribution to the world's destiny. And then our will can work in harmony with the will of God for the redemption of the world from the law of death to the. vision of eternal life. This is the glorious destiny in store for us, the vision of eternity. But it is not accomplished by elevating thoughts and good-will alone, important as these are in sustaining us in our travail day by day. What is required is the courage to travel the path that leads to God, and to bring the world's darkness with us. The prize is a will free from all concerns other than the service of God. In this service alone is the darkness lightened and purpose revealed, as much as we can grasp in our present state of development.

The less developed the person, the more is he the plaything of impersonal forces, and so he is the prisoner of predestination. The more he grows through experience in mind and spirit, the more can he cope with predestined factors as his free will starts a fresh chapter in the world's progress and evolution to spiritual reality. But, exalting as this prospect of spiritual growth may be, we are left with the problem of the many who remain undeveloped. Is their mental and psychological impotence predestined by a capricious God who has decreed their destruction, or are they too worthy of salvation? If the latter is the case – as I devoutly hope it to be – we are bound to posit an existence of the essential personality in the unknown realms beyond physical death, where the present sinful life may be amended by future adventures in the constant light of God's love. But, as we have already seen, the impetus must arise from the creature, in whatever form he may assume in the life beyond death.

3

Seduction

Over the still waters of human happiness there broods an ever-present menace. While everything goes smoothly, almost mechanically, on the surface, there are troubled currents underneath. In fact, the happiness of the surface is sustained by our failing to face the larger issues of life and death that loom in front of us and refuse to be swept away by any mortal expertise. And then comes the storm: the ease and comfort are shattered and we have suddenly to contend for our very lives. The trouble may have an interior source in the form of progressive bodily illness, or it may be a family problem or else a larger issue involving the community, the nation or even the entire world. If disaster has no other merit, it at least sharpens our awareness and brings us closer to reality, which can be defined in our limited existence as the urgency of the present moment. And so, like the sailors in a ship, we can be at one moment on the crest of a wave of prosperity and the next battling for life in the all-encompassing waves of extinction. To most of us the particular disaster that had brought us close to death would itself be the dark face of reality but, in fact, it is merely an outer expression of something far deeper and more menacing. Without what may be called a reactive darkness, we would not be able to appreciate the light of day, just as Adam and Eve never appreciated the bliss of heaven until they were ejected from it. In the well-known words of William Blake in *Auguries of Innocence*,

> Man was made for Joy and Woe
> And when this we rightly know
> Through the World we safely go.
> Joy and Woe are woven fine,
> A Clothing for the Soul divine,
> Under every grief and pine
> Runs a joy with silken twine.

Once there has been an assimilation into our personality of all our life's experiences, good and bad, shameful and discreditable no less than praiseworthy and noble, we are at last qualified to enter into a greater life of the soul where we can be of positive help to many people. Then we neither judge in condemnation nor condescend in complacent virtue but rather enter fully into the soul experience of our fellows.

While things go well for us we can relax, trusting in our own competence guided by the wisdom of our time, mirrored in the smooth running of our community and endorsed by the practice of conventional religion. It certainly is a good thing to keep on the right side of God, as Job himself felt at the beginning of his saga – and he after all was a perfectly righteous man! But constant piety, even if sincere, does not necessarily protect us against the inroads of evil forces – as far as we can discriminate evil from good, which was the initial temptation to which our first ancestors fell, according to the Creation story.

To the impotence of virtue the burden of Job's sufferings bears eloquent witness, as do the lives of all the world's great martyrs for the sake of truth. Nor do the wonders of modern science and technology, or contemporary social understanding and psychology, help the person come to terms with his inner dereliction. All these are of use on an essentially rational level, but they fail lamentably to restore the wounded person who lies floundering in a sea of despair, in which there appears to be no beacon to show the way forward.

It is at this fateful juncture that the forces of darkness show their full power. They enter the scene insidiously disguised as angels of light intent on saving the shattered victim and leading him to the true light. The contract is ludicrously simple: leave everything to us and follow us in faith. We will lead you to health, prosperity and power such as you never dreamed of in the earlier days of your childish innocence. The temptation to throw one's life open to the obliging powers of darkness and trust to what is fondly believed to be God's providence, is enormous. In times of peace and general prosperity such a renunciation of the will to outside agencies would seem inconceivable, but in the face of persistent misfortune, the victim's confidence is severely tried. There is an instinctive reaching out towards anything that affords immediate support, for readily available security is vitally important, but the personality is in constant jeopardy of being offered up to vast impersonal forces whose effects are invariably baneful even if the agent of succour is sincere in his desire to be of help.

The most dramatic illustration of temptation, its

power and the spiritual response to it, is the account of Jesus' trials in the wilderness to which he had been led away by the Holy Spirit. After a long period of fasting, which left him famished, the devil placed three temptations in front of him. In the account of the Fall, Adam and Eve were successfully seduced away from the obedience due to God to a covetousness of personal power: reverence for the Father gave way to naked self-assertiveness. In the account of Jesus, though the plot was more complicated, there was the same underlying theme of self-aggrandisement to the point of usurping his Father's primacy. Then he could, in the form of a human, claim the divine title by virtue of his own power. And so he was challenged successively to turn stones into bread to satisfy his hunger, to throw himself from the temple parapet in order to prove his ascendancy over the natural law and his command of the angelic hosts, and finally to assume world dominion at the price of submitting to the prince of darkness.

It is of note that Jesus, like Elisha, possessed miraculous powers of supply in order to feed his hungry fellows. He could also control the tempestuous elements of the weather when he intervened to calm a storm at sea. But on both these occasions he acted out of compassion and not to assert his personal sovereignty which, in fact, he strove to keep secret lest he be hailed simply as a national saviour or a spectacular miracle worker. He was the humble son of man who was also the Son of God, whose work it was to bring the Kingdom of Heaven closer to the troubled people around him. Far from exalting himself to a high seat of power, in all his marvellous works it was his body that was sacrificed; as St Paul writes, "He was rich, but for your sake he became poor, so that through his poverty you might become rich" (2 Corinthians 8:9). No work of mercy, no act of healing, takes place without an exchange of physical and psychical energy. God is the ultimate source of that energy, which is a product of life itself. He lavishes it prodigally on his children, who usually respond only with coarse insensitivity by abusing it and then indignantly casting the consequences of this desecration in God's face with gestures of aggrieved disappointment. Each day the fragrance of the earth's atmosphere is soiled by man's unclean thoughts and sordid passions. The individual who is left with little manifest hope, as after a period of testing in a situation of failure and tragedy, is especially vulnerable to the dark forces within his own mind, which are nourished by the psychic disorder emitted by the careless crowds. All this seems to be an extension, indeed a materialization, of the evil emanations in the intermediate psychic realm from their primary source in the fallen angelic, or demonic, hierarchies. But here we move beyond tangible human knowledge and are guided intuitively by the Holy Spirit to discern truths at vastly different levels from the cosy rational world of everyday life. In the course of casual conversation all this has a rather far-fetched, dramatic air to it, but to those involved in the deeper world of temptation and conflict, the evil can be sensed to have cosmic implications far beyond the psychological or social mechanisms through which it manifests itself.

Christ repelled the devil because he was filled with the power of God which we call the Holy Spirit. We too can be infused with that power if we live close to the divine presence day by day; the prerequisites are prayer, chastity in relationships, and service to others. But if we rely on the riches of this world for our support, we shall soon find ourselves bereft and powerless in the face of overwhelming temptation. And then our shaky will to good can easily be overridden by inner subversion harnessed to outer coercion. The chastity of which I speak is not to be seen as a purely negative withdrawal from intimate relationships, but rather such an openness to God that human relationships lose their obsessive intensity and predatory undercurrent. Furthermore, chastity should be a way of life relating to eating habits, work, entertainments, and especially conversation, no less than genital sexuality. The chaste person has a will in exquisite readiness for the next moment, whereas the promiscuous individual is so crammed with desire that his will is flabby and inert. "The hungry he has satisfied with good things, the rich sent empty away" (Luke 1:53).

And what is the will? It is the manifest action of the soul or true self, which in turn is defined as the seat of inner identity that shows itself in moral discrimination, aesthetic appreciation and spiritual aspiration. In the soul's "centre" is the spirit which is in contact with the Holy Spirit – indeed, the Spirit of God is immanent in the spirit of man in the soul's centre. It is not surprising that when the lust and corruption of the flesh and the world overwhelm the personality, the will is perverted and the person becomes the chattel of a galaxy of unconscious drives from within and dominating directives from outside. The dark face of reality neutralizes the freely acting will, so that the individual becomes one of a faceless mob that betrays its divine lineage and rushes blindly towards an animal-herd stampede that leads to a destruction of all that is upright and noble. The will can determine its course of action, but only the enlightened will chooses eternal life in God, because it lives in an atmosphere of unremitting love. The spiritual conflict is in essence a battle for the allegiance of the will.

The agent that subverts the will and nullifies its independent action is significantly called the Antichrist. Its most sinister presentation is that of a powerful, apparently well-intentioned person who exacts absolute obedience as a price for his philanthropy. But the demand is insidious and initially unobtrusive: he turns up when an individual, or a group, or even a nation is in sore straits. He is able to alleviate the personal malady or solve the national problem so that an awe-inspiring aura of omniscience surrounds him. He obligingly assumes the mantle of oracle, prophet and guide whose gifts and insights can pre-empt the future and lead to restoration and glory. Furthermore, up to this point there is no discernible evil intent; Jesus Christ himself could fit into the category. Admittedly his riches were spiritual rather than worldly, but enormous store was laid on his utterances and even on his presence as a focus for healing. But then we read the crucial text of John 16:7: "Nevertheless I tell you the truth: it is for your good that I am leaving you. If I do not go, your Advocate will not come, whereas if I go, I will send him to you." Later, in verse 12, we read that there was much that Jesus could say to them, but the burden would be too great for them at that point in time. It was the work of the Advocate, whom we know as the Holy Spirit, to guide them into all the truth.

And so the prophet knows when to leave so that the disciples can proceed with their own lives in greater freedom; they will certainly have gained much from their contact with the teacher, but then they themselves have to put the teaching into practice. His spirit illuminates them, so that their nature is transformed from dross to gold, and then, in spiritual communion with him in God, they can grow into mature people and continue the ministry of the Master. All this takes time: twenty centuries have elapsed since the Incarnation, and even today the Christian community is scarcely out of its childhood! But in every generation a new prophetic voice cries out the truth, and the faithful respond by a deepening of purpose and a broadening of character. This shows itself in a capacity to love more intensely. The risen Christ is never far away, but he has to be called upon in prayer; he does not assert his authority over future generations. He bids us welcome in outflowing acceptance, in the thought of George Herbert's beautiful poem *Love*. He stands knocking at the door of the soul in the words of Revelation 3:20, but he does not come into our lives until we respond by listening, hearing and inviting him to enter. And so the will is exercised in responding to the call – or deliberately ignoring it if we remain proud and unyielding. God does not invade our personalities, since it is his purpose that we should play our part in our own way in the maintenance of the cosmic order. Why this should be so is, needless to say, a mystery to us, creatures of dust who are here today and gone tomorrow. But perhaps our unique individuality, God's special gift to each one of us, enables us to provide a special talent for the use of the corporate body of rational intelligence. Whatever may be the reason, there is no doubt that the human is immensely privileged to be endowed with a mental brilliance and spiritual capacity of such an order as to enter into a creative relationship with God, playing his part as assistant as well as beneficiary. But the privilege brings with it responsibilities, and if the will to co-operation is perverted, the creative process can be severely disrupted.

Unlike the true servant of God, the Antichrist refuses to let his fellows go on their own way. He clings tenaciously to all who have been attracted to him, so that his apparent goodwill becomes a subtle stranglehold on an increasing number of victims. Furthermore, the power wielded by the Antichrist does not depend only on positive achievements; there is also a strong undercurrent of hatred that encourages the victims to follow the course prescribed by the evil one. They begin to see how their illness or national humiliation was the result of the perverse actions and wicked machinations of individuals, groups or classes opposed to their freedom. And so the leaders of sinister cults indoctrinate their followers against their families – whose only intention, it is alleged, was to diminish and exploit them. Or else it may be a social class, a religious group or an ethnic minority that is suspected of aiming at national, or international, supremacy. Such a group is always vulnerable because its life style marks it out as different from the remainder of the community, and if, in addition, many of its members are intellectually gifted and financially successful, the jealousy they evoke is soon rationalized to a suspicion of dishonesty, fraud and criminal intent. Those whom we instinctively fear very soon become the targets of virulent obloquy and later hysterical physical assault. It is suggested to the people by the Antichrist figure that the objects singled out for hatred, by their inbred covetousness, are plotting to take over the community, or else, if they are sexual deviants, by their sinister connections are planning to corrupt the youth of the country. The vulnerability of minorities always makes them special victims of the force of evil that dwells in all of us – including, of course, the minority group. They, victims though they may become through the jealous suspicion of their neighbours, are animated by the same forces. This is part of the great power of the Antichrist. In the end all the people may be corrupted, except for the saints on whose witness humanity survives and grows painfully into a greater reality of purpose.

The powers of evil from without work by activating the springs of hatred that lie deep in the psyche. Just as we would not seek God if we did not contain something of the divine nature within ourselves enabling us to identify the source of all goodness, so we would not respond to temptation were the need not already there, dormant and waiting to be satisfied. The type of person who prides himself on his virtue, rather like the Pharisee in the famous parable of Luke 18:9–14, is especially vulnerable to the attack of the evil one. The reason for this is not his hypocrisy, which can easily be unmasked and dissipated by a robust sense of humour, but his ignorance of his inner disorder. This inner disorder we all harbour, but nothing can conceal it from our notice so successfully as self-righteous piety acting in concert with a judgemental denunciation of all that falls beneath it. Below this imposing edifice the foundations are not infrequently rotten with lust, avarice and resentment, vices that are, to a greater or lesser extent, festering in us all until a situation arises in which we are able to see what is happening and take appropriate measures to deal with the trouble. But the moralistic type of person is so entranced by his own excellence that he sees no need to look any further into himself – and when he finds a less acceptable type of person succeeding materially, he becomes increasingly jealous. If, like the Pharisee of the parable, he has no deeper love for humanity, he will seethe at the prosperity of the wicked, a reaction we all share to a greater or lesser extent. Psalm 73 is a graphic account of the anguished meditation of a good man on the success of scoundrels, but in the end he comforts himself with the reflection that the evil ones have their final reward in destruction, whereas he, the just man, looks forward to fellowship with God in a relationship that makes all worldly pleasures trivial by comparison. This is excellent as far as it goes, but can we dismiss our erring fellows for ever? Can there be a lasting union with God in a heaven that is exclusive of so much human nature?

In the Parable of the Publican and the Pharisee the completely unworthy sinner, as he approaches God in the temple, suddenly has a blinding awareness of his own wretchedness, and commends himself to God's mercy in pure faith. He is accepted because God's nature is love, and we can safely believe that God's love dwelt subsequently in him so that his life could thenceforth be directed to serving his fellow creatures and not exploiting them. By contrast, the Pharisee, while exulting in his own righteousness, could contemptuously reject the squalid publican alongside him at prayer. We could only too easily imagine the Pharisee's indignation if a member of the lower orders, such as the publican, started to prosper. All the morally disciplined man's virtues would appear to have been of little avail in life's race, and soon the darkness within would well up uncontrollably. As it could never be tolerated in the consciousness of the Pharisee, it would soon be projected as hatred on to the publican and his many peers in our morally ambivalent society. It is at this point that the Antichrist would be so welcome a figure – and he in turn would enlist the self-righteous person eagerly for his own work of destruction. The scapegoat delineated by the evil one would in this way be a most welcome target on which to discharge all the pent-up, though unacknowledged, venom of the masses.

In this context one can meditate only in fascinated horror on how the Germans, possibly the most civilized people in the world, were so seduced by an agent of evil intent that they descended to a barely conceivable barbarity, of an order that could have destroyed the roots of society had it succeeded in its terrible purpose. The tragedy started with the German defeat in the First World War, a bitter pill for a very proud, martial nation to swallow. In addition, the Versailles treaty showed no mercy on the vanquished: the victors were intent on the complete humiliation of the Germans and their allies. The attempts at a new order of peace founded in the League of Nations were futile, as the League showed its impotence to enforce any order, and in addition a terrible economic depression hit Europe and America in the period of the early thirties. Few countries suffered more severely than Germany, where the rate of inflation galloped to unprecedented heights. Successive governments failed to make an impression on the economic situation, and finally the country was seduced by a demonic demagogue, Adolf Hitler, who offered a fresh hope with his revolutionary policies. He preached national redemption with a society modelled on the heroes of Wagnerian opera, while the darkness lying behind this imposing façade was projected on to the character of an especially vulnerable group, the Jews, who were far too successful in their undertakings and therefore easily accused of draining the German economy of its resources. The Jews had been, until the establishment of their own state of Israel, the perennial international scapegoat because of their amazing capacity to succeed materially, their religious exclusiveness, and their dependence on the goodwill of the countries where they lived. When all was going well they were tolerated, even esteemed, but in times of depression all the troubles could so conveniently be attributed to the traditional slander of their scheming dishonesty. Furthermore, there were other figures of detestation also in the Nazi state: gypsies, Jehovah's Witnesses, Communists, mental defectives and homosexuals, to name the most prominent. Each group was loathed because of its distinctive ethos that cut across the fierce uniformity demanded of the regenerated German people.

Even more terrible was the almost unanimous assent conferred on the regime, especially in its early years of government before the Second World War. At this time, both Catholic and Lutheran churchmen gave their tacit – and often explicit – support, while the professional bodies expelled Jewish members. The medical profession was soon to perform experiments on Jews and gypsies in preference to animals: animal experimentation was banned early in the course of the regime, but no such prohibition extended to the human species. Of course, before one condemns the approval of the German people outright, one has to acknowledge the skill of Hitler in radically reducing the unemployment figures, building imposing motorways and restoring national morale. But he also built up, quite illicitly under the terms of the Versailles treaty, a gigantic military machine. The aim of this was ostensibly to regain lost territory but in fact to attain world domination, so that the ideals of Nazism could be fulfilled internationally. The fate of the Jews in German-occupied countries during the Second World War is a potent reminder of what this meant in terms of human suffering. And yet, as we have already noted, there was general assent for a very long time, even among practising Christians, perhaps due to a basic culpable indifference if not actual malice. None so blind as those who will not see! And the Antichrist blinds men's vision, just as Christ restores sight to the blind.

Hitler's minister of propaganda, Joseph Goebbels, enunciated a telling general law: the greater the lie, the more readily will it be believed. Once it resonates with the emotional needs of the hearer it will ignite the fuel of his prejudice to a scarcely extinguishable flame of enthusiasm. The same principle holds for racism, sexism, and the acceptance (and also the rejection) of the objective reality of psychic phenomena. It is our emotional nature, the "feeling" function of Carl G. Jung, that is our Achilles' heel; through it the forces of evil can strike at the root of our personality. But, of course, it is also sensitive to beauty and the pain of those around us, and can be the way of release from selfish preoccupation to a greater concern for other people. The person who is at the mercy of his emotions is a great public menace; when he can control them from a higher spiritual centre, they can become the inspiration of enormous aesthetic and altruistic creativity. Then they fertilize the active will and can lead to a glorious flowering of the personality.

"Whom Jupiter wishes to destroy he first makes mad", was the way James Duport put it. But the powers of evil are most probably the fallen angelic hosts now imbued with demonic zeal, and they can unleash the dark forces in all of us, whether on a personal, communal, national or international level. The ultimate madness is a rush – like that of the Gadarene swine, into whom malign forces entered after a famous healing by Jesus – of the people to a destructive fury that finds its end in a hatred so intense that nothing less than the total extermination of the abomination will suffice. In a less dramatic, more common way none of us is exempt from feelings of hatred; if we fondly believe that we are "above all that sort of thing", circumstances will soon arise in our personal lives that serve to dispel any such delusion. To move towards a state beyond mortal desire was the Buddha's prescription for the attainment of the life free from suffering that finds its end in the transpersonal bliss of Nirvana. But in fact we cannot move beyond desire until we have experienced it and fallen victim to its noxious embrace. Only then can the desire itself be redeemed from selfish indulgence to communal charity. There was one, Jesus Christ, who, though truly beyond mortal desire inasmuch as the Godhead dwelt fully within him, nevertheless, at the time of his baptism, voluntarily took on himself all mortal desires, and in so doing revealed the way towards their transcendence. The way is the antithesis of hatred, which finds its end in total darkness; it is the slow, painful way of love that, to quote 1 Corinthians 13:4–8, is patient, kind, meek, unselfish and slow to take offence. On the contrary, it keeps no score of wrongs nor does it gloat over others' sins. It delights in the truth and there is nothing it cannot face. There is no limit to its faith, hope and endurance. Above all these qualities, it never comes to an end. The end of hatred is the destruction of the loathed object; the end of love is its transformation in the divine image; God is both the foundation of love and its end. But love is more than a liberal sentimentality. It follows a full crucifixion of the personal life, so that all desires are seen to be fatuous except the desire to know and serve God – and therefore the creation – as completely as one can.

But even an earnest desire to serve the created order can go wrong. Once again, the events in the twentieth century give us food for reflection. The Antichrist is mutable in form and can assume many unlikely appearances.

4

The Noonday Plague

Psalm 91 assures us that in God's keeping we shall not fear the hunter's trap by night nor the arrow that flies by day, the pestilence that stalks in darkness nor the plague raging at noonday. If we were to transpose these situations to the hell of the twentieth century, the hunter's nocturnal trap could be likened to the Nazi secret police, who knocked on the doors of the houses of their victims in the middle of the night: their footsteps instilled panic in all who lived there. The daytime arrow could be associated with the cowardly attack by a "freedom-fighting" terrorist. The pestilence stalking in the darkness would find its manifestation in dread venereal diseases, notably AIDS, that followed indiscreet sexual exposure, or drug addiction with its degrading effect on the personality. But what about the noonday plague? It could easily be identified as the darkness of perdition masquerading as the light of reason sufficient to deceive all but those whose sight was clear and unobstructed.

The prince of darkness identified as the Antichrist works to perfection when he espouses causes of moral rectitude. He then affects a guise of virtuousness, and the populace can project all their own unconscious darkness on to the special targets of their execration. The social activist, for example, works, at least to his own satisfaction, for the alleviation of injustice and the fair apportionment of resources. The end in distant view is the truly egalitarian society echoing Karl Marx's words, "From each according to his abilities, to each according to his needs". The vision of this earthly Utopia is so splendid that its very brilliance shields the inner sight from contact with the difficulties in the way of its fulfilment. Instead of a candid, truthful appraisal of the facts, the blame is categorically laid on the shoulders of a special class or income group. On these privileged people – now rendered in vengeance lamentable in the extreme – full blame and opprobrium are heaped. Once again the Antichrist has attained a stunning victory by filling the world with hatred, but this time in the cause of social justice. If the fascist way is primarily one of virulent persecution of defenceless racial groups, so that its underlying evil is apparent to all uncommitted people who use their native powers of discernment, the communist approach is much more subtle. It affects, even to its own conviction, concern for the underprivileged members of society. But it acts essentially to undermine and ruthlessly destroy all that opposes its views, and this in the name of solidarity with the masses. There are few more persuasive ways of world domination than this, since its visionary message appeals to the hearts of all men of goodwill. So they become guileless sponsors of a new society no longer controlled by the power of the mighty rich. But the whole population is often sadly diminished in the heat of the transaction. We often unleash the worst evil when we are intent on serving a favourite cause, for the ego consciousness tends to take command, dictating how matters should proceed and how any opposition is to be met, crushed and eliminated. This, to the lesser extent, often occurs in the pursuance of personal objectives. How much more terrible does it become when matters of political importance are involved, whether local, national or international!

And this is the root of the evil: it lies not in the cause so much as in the people who control it. A cause, after all, is an idealistic mental construction, as full of glory as the Tower of Babel that ambitious men were all set to complete. It, in itself, may contain the seeds of enormous philanthropic vision, but it is corrupted by the darkness lying in its founders. The uncomfortable observation that strikes the dispassionate reader of *Mein Kampf*, Hitler's blueprint of the ideal Germany he aimed at creating, is the moral rectitude of so much of his vision. The sad degeneracy of the Germany of that time was so intolerable to any right-minded person that the Nazi scheme, aimed at the restoration of traditional values by a radical regime of self-discipline and national regeneration, seemed so obviously right. Such self-discipline seems very clearly preferable to self-indulgence, until we begin to look behind the noble mask at the hideously poised devil grinning with the face of unmitigated evil. Then the truth shows itself uncompromisingly: discipline can be the most dangerous type of indulgence when it simply boosts the individual so that he feels superior to the lesser mortals who still grope in the mud of flesh and blood. How much more dangerous indeed is the complacent, righteous Pharisee than the degraded publican in Jesus' famous parable – and that even before the publican's conversion to God in a blinding awareness of truth! It is evident that the Antichrist can pervert that which is basically good, as well as harness the evil emotions that lie dormant in all of us. It is no surprise that a number of Jesus' parables exalt the sinner above the coldly virtuous person, the loose-liver above the morally scrupulous. The sinner has the potentiality for repentance and healing when he comes to himself in abject humiliation; the virtuous person, without the experience of life in its manifold dimensions, can live so comfortably in his ivory tower of excellence that he is impervious to the grace of God and therefore the love of his fellow creatures. Indeed, his moral excellence *is* his god, which ousts the Living God from his life. It is such a person who is especially liable to explode in violence when his manifest goodness seems to bear scant reward, and then the devil enters the vacuum and wreaks enormous violence and havoc. We have already considered the shadow that lives in all of us as a concatenation of savage impulses barely kept in control by a superimposed moral prerogative, but liable to erupt at any moment when we feel cheated or rejected by life, so that we can blame other people for our discomfiture and humiliation.

Is virtue then to be derided? Are the loose-living members of society our paradigm of the good life? Surely not, but we have to distinguish between a virtuousness based on the complacency of a comfortable life style far removed from the temptations of the multitude, and one that springs from compassion and humility. The first is cold and can easily be taken over by the dark forces. The second is of Christ and works towards the healing of the world even to its own death, remembering that the greatest love is prepared to give up its life for its friend. And love of this order transcends individual persons while embracing them all in a totality of relationship. In other words, when we know truly how to love, no creature can be excluded from that love. It is this thought that convinces me that all material things are fashioned in order to be resurrected into eternal life by the One alone whose creative Word brought the cosmos itself into existence. Love cannot exclude anything from its caring, no matter how unreceptive the beloved one may be.

How different all this is from the terrible history of the communist revolution in Russia! It aimed at eradicating the appalling cruelty of the Tsarist regime (allied to a compliant national church). This tended to concentrate all the resources in the hands of a powerful ruling class. But the revolution was also cruel; its zenith was the horror of the dictatorship of Stalin, whose brutality far outdistanced anything the people had previously experienced. It is estimated that the dictator killed about seventeen million people, which makes Hitler's murder of six million Jews a quite moderate slaughter by comparison! All who disagreed with Stalin's policies, including the peasant class (the kulaks), were mercilessly destroyed. The dictator was quoted as saying that scum populations do not disappear voluntarily, a sentiment that his ideological adversary Hitler would have heartily endorsed. But the most revealing evidence of the Russian dictator's perfidy is embodied in the terrible "purges" of his peers that he engineered during the period of the thirties. They were all forced to confess to crimes of disloyalty under conditions of subtle torture, and then brought to public trial where they were convicted of treason, much to the righteous indignation of the spectators, before being shot dead. One of the most important novels of our time, *Darkness at Noon* by Arthur Koestler, describes the procedures of these "Moscow trials" in stark detail. He wrote out of inside knowledge of the events, not merely from an author's fertile imagination. In the end the most auspicious founders of the communist state could be persuaded to admit their complicity in the most compromising acts of treason. But one of the most potent allies of the torturing inquisitors was the guilty conscience of the accused: they too had earlier connived at the deaths of colleagues whose common decency had caused them to question the morality of a state that showed arrant duplicity in its relations with fascist groups in the west. Indeed, there is a telling point of contact between agents of the extreme right and the extreme left. This is their mutual disregard for all moral scruples in the pursuance of the immediate advantage for their cause. Expediency determines morality in their scheme of action.

And so we read of the central character of the book, Rubashov, carrying on a communication with his neighbour, a royalist counter-revolutionary, in a code of graded taps on the wall of his cell. He is, in fact, the only decent character in the novel apart from the old porter, Wassilij, still a Christian albeit a clandestine one, who remembered Rubashov as the bearded Partisan-commander of the days of the revolution, before his meteoric rise to national distinction as one of the leaders of the government. Now he has fallen out of favour with the leader, and is subjected to three trials, whose outcome is a foregone conclusion, before his inevitable execution. In the course of the tapping conversation the man of traditional allegiance defines honour as the willingness to live and die for one's belief. To this Rubashov responds with derision: honour, to him, is to be useful without vanity. The one equates honour with decency, the other with usefulness. Rubashov further declares that the regime has replaced decency by reason, and he apparently approves of this change, at least at that point in his trial. Subsequently he is to be interrogated by Gletkin, the personification of all torturers throughout the ages of men's belief. He has his counterpart in the officials who questioned Jesus prior to handing him over to Pilate, and the inquisitors who did not flinch from breaking a heretic's body in the service of his immortal soul – and also that of the Catholic Church. His cold brutality is unfortunately typical of the demeanour of intense, humourless people who are prepared to save the world according to their private beliefs. He defines truth as what is useful to humanity, whereas falsehood is what is harmful. But in both this definition, and that of Rubashov, the human is acting without any special reference to the divine principle and therefore perhaps impeding it. Are we any closer to the enigma of sorting out the fruit of the knowledge of good and evil now than in the days of our allegorical ancestors Adam and Eve? In the contemporary dictatorial mode moral values are compromised without scruple for the sake of expediency, and the human is demoted to the role of a computer that can be programmed to respond to the demands of his immediate superiors who, in turn, direct their loyalty to those in higher authority. This is the way of life of the person who has turned his back on the divine image within himself, and works with bovine indifference to the higher calling of the human race. This calling has been shown to us in the lives and teachings of the world's spiritual geniuses throughout the ages.

But Koestler himself quotes a terrible passage from *De schismate libri III*, written by Dietrich von Nieheim in 1411:

> When the existence of the Church is threatened, she is released from the commandments of morality. With unity as the end, the use of every means is sanctified, even cunning, treachery, violence, simony, prison, death. For all order is for the sake of the community, and the individual must be sacrificed to the common good.

Nieheim was Bishop of Verden, and he had no doubt that the Church embraced the common good so absolutely as to be inseparable from it. The same argument would undoubtedly have been used by Hitler, Stalin and every "freedom-fighting" terrorist that stalked the earth. It is terrible to find the Church included in such company, but the truth cannot be evaded. The Antichrist has been especially active in the counsels of the Christian faith since her leaders aligned themselves with the political power of the defunct Roman Empire, which thenceforth was described as Holy. The third temptation of Christ in the wilderness, to attain absolute worldly dominion at the price of worshipping the prince of the world who is the devil himself, though successfully parried by the Lord, was not so easily withstood by his distant heirs some four hundred years later. And the devil laughed as the prelates fondly believed they had attained the means of a universal proclamation of the Faith and a subsequent enforcement of it. It was the power that inflamed their passions rather than the Cross that chastened their souls. In the celebrated words of the first Baron Acton, "Power tends to corrupt, and absolute power corrupts absolutely".

Yet without power nothing is achieved, and an other-worldly Church is not only impotent but also complacent. The work is to bring heaven down to earth, in other words to inspire the secular arm with such goodness that the government approaches, at least haltingly, to something of the kingdom of God that Jesus came to proclaim in his great work of healing and deliverance. Jesus taught his apostles unceasingly that the master is the servant of all, that he came on earth to serve and not to be served by others. Those who take the highest places at a banquet are liable to be unceremoniously shifted down in rank as more celebrated guests arrive, whereas the genuinely humble person who, as a matter of custom, abases himself, will be exalted. Indeed, as we enter the kingdom of God all thoughts about personal status recede into the background. A gratitude that we are counted worthy to be present fills us with amazed awe – and then we are overwhelmed to find our peers there also. This delight turns to speechless joy when we find others present whom we would scarcely have recognized in our earthly circumstances. By contrast, the Antichrist inflates our own personalities, making us feel that we are special and above our fellows in importance. Of course, each of us is special in his own right, but our importance depends on the use we make of our unique gifts and talents in this life on earth. Those who seem to be nature's failures, like for instance the mentally defective and those who are born physically incapacitated, have their own contribution to make as pure witnesses who stand and wait in hope.

In the end we should neither covet special favours nor disport an abject humility; both are aspects of self-inflation. We remember Jesus' strictures on those who make a great show of their piety at street-corners and places of worship, who make their pious fasting plain for all the world to see by their gloomy countenances. They are no better than those who trumpet their gifts to charitable causes so that their generosity may be widely known (Matthew 6). We have, by contrast, to forget ourselves sufficiently to serve God in the sanctity of the present moment. In such needle-pointed dedication to the eternal presence of God there is no chink in our spiritual armour where the evil one can gain a foothold. In the promise of the third Beatitude, meekness aimed at having the earth as its possession is a seditious ploy of the ego consciousness. But if the gentle spirit is authentic, it finds itself unimpeded in possession of all things. Needing nothing, it possesses everything. Once we desire any finite quality we immediately exclude the One beyond all qualities, and then the forces of evil find a welcoming point of entry. We remember, ruefully, Jesus' words, "Not everyone who calls me 'Lord, Lord' will enter the kingdom of Heaven, but only those who do the will of my heavenly Father" (Matthew 7:21).

In one of W. Somerset Maugham's later novels,

The Razor's Edge, the narrator envisages Christ repelling the devil's three temptations in the wilderness, but then being confronted by a fourth, far more subtle, one.

He said, "If thou wilt accept shame and disgrace, scourging, a crown of thorns and death on the cross, thou shalt save the human race, for greater love hath no man than this, that a man lay down his life for his friends." Jesus fell, and the devil laughed till his sides ached, for he knew the evil that men would commit in the name of their redeemer.

Maugham goes on to meditate on the cruel wars that Christianity has occasioned, the persecutions, the tortures Christian has inflicted on Christian, the unkindness, the hypocrisy, the intolerance, and he imagines the devil considering the balance sheet with complacency.

And when he remembers that it has laid upon mankind the bitter burden of the sense of sin that has darkened the beauty of the starry night and cast a baleful shadow on the passing pleasures of a world to be enjoyed, he must chuckle as he murmurs: Give the devil his due.

This condemnation, coming from an agnostic with an acute sense of the divine mystery almost too acute for him to solve his metaphysical problems by a simple submission to any dogmatic faith, should give the believer food for thought. Provided we are open to new insights, our faith will never stagnate, and the Holy Spirit's work of leading us into the progressive revelation of truth will not be thwarted. The sense of sin is real and not to be avoided. It tells us how far we miss the mark of goodness and love day by day in our personal relationships and the work we do. The pagan way has, at its best, a great and poignant beauty, but it ends on a note of extinction. By contrast, the Christian way explores the depths of the personality where sin finds its home, and it works towards the redemption of the whole personality from the thraldom to sinful impulses. The Christian way proceeds to a resurrection of all creatures in the light of God.

But the accusation of the masochistic delight that many Christians have taken in the crucifixion event, which has far too often been projected as unashamed sadism on unacceptable groups, is too near the mark to be evaded. The emotions that are aroused by the horror of Jesus' crucifixion can so easily find their outlet in attacks on Jews, whose forebears were culpably involved in this terrible miscarriage of justice. In the Middle Ages, and later too, the inhabitants of the Jewish quarters of many cities (the original ghettos) were the victims of savage assaults after the Sacred Liturgy of Good Friday. It is much easier to dwell on the pain of the crucifixion than the forgiveness inherent in Jesus' appearance to the feeble, ungrateful disciples after his resurrection. He came to renew his relationship with them as a preliminary to their continuing his work after his ascension and the pentecostal infusion of the Holy Spirit upon and within them. So here again a nobility of purpose that far outdistances the Marxist ideal at its most radiant can also be the point of entry of the dark forces of hatred poised to destroy everything that stands in the path of the vision. Where both the Christian and

Marxist ways fail is in the moral inadequacy of their followers: fervent professions of belief do not automatically lead to holiness. But where the atheistic Marxist fondly believes that economic reorganization can change the face of society from darkness to light, the Christian is starkly aware of the inherent tendency to corruption, deeply embedded in the human psyche. This "original sin" certainly shows itself in corrupt political institutions and economic practices, but these cannot be finally healed until there is a repentance, a change of mind (or metanoia), in the individual as well as in the wider community. This follows an openness to God in prayer, for we are justified, or brought into right relationship with God, by faith and not works. These succeed the inflow of the Holy Spirit, and are directed by love not self-centredness.

Such, at any rate, is the basis of truly Christian action, but the history of the Faith, as Somerset Maugham reflects, is less inspiring. This is because, from the time of Ananias and Sapphira, the Christian psyche has been flawed by material interests that have insidiously usurped the place of God as the central focus of life, instead of remaining in their proper peripheral situation. The Incarnation has set in motion a quite new dispensation which is to quicken the process of human development, but it has taken many centuries of painful self-knowledge for the humble disciple to grasp the full measure of this change and to strive to act accordingly. It is not sufficient to affirm Jesus' divinity according to impressive credal formulae. Until that divinity is actualized in the life of the believer, filled with God's grace, his menacing shadow side is left unheeded, and is liable to be projected on to anyone of independent judgement and action who threatens the security inherent in his understanding of the Faith. In other words, Christ's sacrifice of himself to reconcile the world to God can remain a comfortable theological construction under which to take shelter while jettisoning one's hatred on to those who have independent views about the nature of Christ and reality. But that sacrifice can also be the means of growth whereby one eventually attains something of the stature of Christ in one's own being. At this juncture bitter theological dispute gives way to the presence of the Lord in one's life, as love takes precedence over thought. And then the enlightened thinking process blossoms into a theology of resurrection that works towards a reconciliation of opposed tendencies which would previously have warred destructively against one another.

The destructive encounter between the mother religion, Judaism, and its Christian daughter is especially instructive of the way in which the devil can corrupt two very great religious faiths. Christianity itself developed out of an intra-Judaic tragedy in which the forces of darkness used the guardians of the orthodox tradition to bring about the death of the greatest representative of that tradition – and indeed of all traditions that have their end in the vision of God. The Jews assailed the early Christian community uncompromisingly, contemptuously rejecting its belief in the messiahship of Jesus, and pouring scorn on the claims made about his person. In due course, the growing Christian community retaliated with an increasingly virulent hatred against the Jews: the eight infamous sermons preached by St

John Chrysostom at Antioch in A.D. 387 formed a culmination of all previous anti-Judaic (a term preferable to the less precise anti-Semitic) pronouncements by the Church Fathers, and were in a very real way the Christian basis on which Hitler could justify his own unassuageable hostility towards the Jews. When an agreement was struck between the Roman Emperor Constantine and the Christian Church, punitive measures were immediately instituted against the Jews. These measures lasted many centuries; even the father of the Reformation, Martin Luther, followed the Catholic precedent when he was unable to convert the Jews to his particular system. James Parkes, a modern protagonist of Judeo-Christian reconciliation (himself an Anglican priest), has compared the violence and obscenity of Luther's *Die Juden und Ihre Lügen* with John Chrysostom's terrible sermons.

The Jews not unnaturally became even more entrenched in their religion with unyielding tenacity. Indeed, any relaxation might have meant a capitulation to the hated Christians. The impasse began to be unblocked at the time of the Enlightenment in the eighteenth century, when Reason had its triumph over "superstition". Many sensible people discarded formal religious commitment altogether, but this agnosticism was redressed by the Evangelical Revival in Britain and by Hasidism, a mystical development of Judaism, in Eastern Europe. By the nineteenth century political rights had been accorded to Jews in most European countries outside Russia, but the smouldering anti-Judaism in the emotional life of many Gentiles flared up from time to time in personal victimization. The notorious Dreyfus affair in France was a crucial instance: the unjust conviction of a Jewish army officer, Alfred Dreyfus, on a charge of treason, and his savage humiliation and imprisonment, initiated the modern movement of Jews back to Palestine known as Zionism (there had been small migrations of Jews there in previous centuries). It seemed obvious to Zionists that no Jew could expect justice in any country other than his own. Our own century has seen the dénouement of the matter: the German unconscious darkness erupted into demonic Nazism with its massacre of six million European Jews. After the defeat of Hitler and his allies, the conscience of most of the world enabled the Zionist dream to materialize, and the state of Israel came into being in 1948. Now at last the Jews have a solid base of security. But the resident Arab population has suffered grievously as a result of this massive exodus of Jews to their promised land, and we have not yet heard the last of the story.

There seems, however, to be a growing accord between the two religions: Christians are beginning to trace the roots of their tradition more dispassionately, and can acknowledge their debt to the Jews. They are now able to recognize the validity of Judaism in its own right apart from its Christian connection. Jews, on the other hand, are now able to mention the name of "Jesus" without bitterness, and the opprobrium of centuries of Christian persecution is being seen in the broader light of universal human tragedy. But only the finger of God can lead them to a full understanding of the man whose death their ancestors decreed, and which in turn brought such great misery upon future generations of his people. It seems that Jew and Christian alike have some distance to travel before either will recognize the face of their Messiah.

The quest for truth inspires all spiritual action. Only when we can accept the fact that truth is never confined to one religion alone, any more than to a particular political ideology, can we become free, and then our will attains a real power to decide according to our own unclouded vision. But when an ideology is identified categorically with the truth, God is gradually eased out as the dogma replaces his presence. And then the Antichrist can come in obligingly to fill the void. Whenever we are set in our ways and refuse to follow the leading of the Holy Spirit to a new appreciation of reality, we begin to decay, and darkness finds an easy entry into our souls. The statement of Jesus, "If you dwell within the revelation I have brought, you are indeed my disciples; you shall know the truth and the truth will set you free" (John 8:31–32), is the heart of the matter. This knowledge is not an objective understanding of God so much as an intimate relationship with him, the unitive knowledge of love such as the parents of especially beloved children had at the time of their conception. We think of Abraham and Sarah giving birth to Isaac, or Zechariah and Elizabeth to John the Baptist. In that love all future endeavours find their blessing, and fear of change is cast out.

When Rubashov is finally about to be shot, it is the royalist facing eighteen more years of imprisonment who encourages him with his taps on the wall of his cell. He makes the period of waiting for the arrival of the executioner tolerable as he diverts Rubashov's attention from his imminent execution by light, yet pertinent observations about imaginary future activities and present comfort. He is the only human being in the prison, because he has not allowed his personality to be warped by his gaolers. He has retained his humanity, whereas the servants of the regime are now mere automata without any apparent soul structure. We remember Jesus' warning, in Matthew 10:28, about those who are able to destroy both soul and body in hell, as opposed to the relative harmlessness of those who kill the body, but cannot kill the soul. Whether the soul would be eternally destroyed is a matter of debate, inasmuch as God is in command of all his creation, and his nature is love, but it is certain that the work of the Antichrist is to wreak such havoc on man's inner nature that he may cease for a very long time to be an independently functioning person. The royalist retained an authentic soul despite his sufferings, the secret being his inner faith and integrity of purpose. Rubashov attained something of this stature by virtue of his contact with the heroic protester. He was able to die like a man and not a craven, hysterical weakling. And yet the regime supported by this royalist protester was absolutely unacceptable, and any nostalgia for its way of life would have been quite out of place. The tragedy lay in the attitude of its Marxist successors to the things of eternity; once these were dismissed as mere bourgeois illusions, the unimpeded force of the ego-centred human could take charge of everything. But the devil within controlled the new élite.

5

The Terror of Madness

Just as the noble aspirations of the French Revolution proceeded with a crescendo of increasing public disorder as its more moderate leaders died, culminating in the reign of the fanatic Robespierre and his supporters with "The Terror", in which numerous heads rolled beneath the guillotine, so injustice, once initiated by the power of arms, rushes both its perpetrators and its victims down a steep slope of violence where both find their end in destruction. Hatred, once fomented, seeks its resolution in such fury that finally no one is left to tell the tale except the Antichrist, the chosen vehicle of the devil, who gloats over the carnage that impassioned men have occasioned – and all in the name of justice. Power in the hands of those possessed of fanatical zeal soon grips them in a bond of satanic strength as more and more of the tradition of the past is shattered and its treasures fed to the flames. The fanatic's obsessional desire to destroy – an innate part of human behaviour designed to cast away soiled and worn-out material which would otherwise accumulate and block the way of the Holy Spirit who makes all things new – now attains gargantuan proportions. In his hatred nothing will suffice except the complete annihilation of the abominated one. In turn, the object of abuse may be forced to cringe in terror at the onslaught, but in due course he will retaliate, and then more destruction will follow.

The sequence is seen often enough in our private lives. If we are cheated, swindled or belittled in any way, we will never be able to let the grievance rest until an innate sense of justice has been satisfied. It is right that this should be so: the fourth Beatitude commends those who seek the triumph of what is right, promising them satisfaction. In uncivilized groups the individual may take matters forthwith into his own hands, but the end result will be destructive to personal relationships and harmful to the communal peace. Where civilization flourishes, the benign, impartial arm of the law can deal with various manifest breaches of justice according to the criminal code; for this we should always be thankful. A free judiciary is a blessing contingent upon a democratic society in which the law is not muzzled by any powerful private or political interest. When a nation has acquired sufficient communal responsibility to be in charge of its own institutions, it has attained a landmark of human dignity, and the power of God is in the ascendant, irrespective of the religious denomination and credal confession of the people. Where God is dismissed as illusory, man soon steps into his place, and then power falls insidiously into the hands of a ruling clique. In other words, the democratic principle works most perfectly when God is given precedence over the human will, for then each of us may learn humility in the day-to-day running of his life in the face of the mystery of creation.

However, the ruling group can enlist God for its support. It can even elevate the Deity to a place of supreme eminence in its sectarian councils, in which case a repressive theocracy will emerge. The history of world religion, both past and present, contains too many examples of this tendency for our comfort. In such a travesty of truth, the god whose aid is invoked is in essence a puppet of the ruling class, which may well include a professional priesthood. But the true God, in whom we live, move and have our existence, is quietly eased out of sight, since his nature is love, light and a purpose far beyond mere self-assertiveness. The will of the true God is the growth of his creatures into that fullness of personality seen in the world's saints. The will of a repressive theocracy is the exaltation of a religious hierarchy at the expense of the remainder of the community, who are exploited by those at the summit of power, but all in the name of God. The result of this abuse of God's name has been the total rejection of religion by many intelligent, sensitive people. Ironically, one of the historical proofs of Christ's authenticity has been the persistence of his witness, despite the crimes committed in his name by those who have counted themselves among his followers. His Church has certainly kept that name alive, but often obscured it and even discredited its integrity when it has claimed his authority from the vantage point of power. It then becomes a focus of injustice against which the populace revolts. The Holy Spirit is the power that ignites the rebellion, but soon his beneficial, life-giving directive is liable to be encroached on by less scrupulous forces of darkness intent upon revenge and destruction.

It follows that both personal and national grievances, if not satisfied, rankle in the hearts of those who suffer, as the unconscious depths become the repository of dark, demonic material from its collective store, which can set in motion enormous havoc. It is far better that these tendencies should be confronted at once and their impact withstood. Their eruption into full consciousness is attended by a sharp outburst of anger, which must in no way be suppressed. The proper manner with which to deal with anger is to acknowledge it without moral judgement, either a feeling of guilt or of self-righteousness. Then one can detach oneself from it and look at it with a degree of objectivity. The help of a skilled counsellor is of the greatest value, since he acts as a sympathetic observer who can both share the emotional discharge and help direct it into more fruitful channels. What can be ameliorated in the field of personal relationships and communal action is open to the reconciliation effected by reason and goodwill working through dialogue or political procedures, as the case may be. It is when these civilized means of communication break down or are impossible to effect that the power of hatred shows itself, and the person or group can easily descend into barbarity. Or they may ascend to a new height of compassion and service.

It is a fearful thing to witness a person consumed with hatred, either because of the misfortune that life itself has visited on him or because of some outside injustice that seems to have hit him so arbitrarily. His entire mental life is dominated by this one theme, so that the pleasures of the present hour pass unnoticed behind the film of venom that infiltrates every thought and action. The present moment, our point of immediate contact with reality, is blurred by the emotional turbidity of the psychic atmosphere, as the person is enveloped in a fog of malice that works to separate his soul from the lifegiving power of the Holy Spirit. It also has the disastrous effect of alienating an increasing number of his friends, who are suspected of treachery if they fail to shun the one who is alleged to be the source of the trouble. If the matter is not dealt with expeditiously, the scarcely-contained, explosive emotional power of hatred wreaks havoc on all those around the person, so that he progressively cuts himself off from fellowship with his peers and ultimately from life itself. In his blind rage he tramples on all that lives, oblivious of the damage he is causing, and caring even less about the pain he is inflicting on everyone around him. Such a person lives in a private world whose form is a battlefield, and all who are not for him in his imaginary war of reparation are counted among his enemies. At any moment the most innocent bystander may be the target for a terrible outburst of abuse. The one who is possessed with hatred is beyond reason, and prayer itself may make no impact on him. One suspects that Hitler fell into this category in respect of his blind, irrational hatred of the Jews. The attitude, one suspects, had some basis in a past unfortunate encounter, but the reaction was out of all proportion and aimed at the total destruction of the entire group. How easy it is for the powers of darkness to use such a person for their own nefarious ends of chaos and extinction! All hatred is of the devil, no matter how justified it may appear, because its end is total destruction of both the hater and the person who is hated.

We remember in this respect Jesus' injunction: "Anyone who nurses anger against his brother must be brought to judgement. If he abuses his brother he must answer for it to the court; if he sneers at him he will have to answer for it in the fires of hell. If, when you are bringing your gift to the altar, you suddenly remember that your brother has a grievance against you, leave your gift where it is before the altar. First go and make peace with your brother, and only then come back and offer your gift" (Matthew 5:22–24). St Paul adds further, "If you are angry, do not let anger lead you into sin; do not let sunset find you still nursing it; leave no loop-hole for the devil" (Ephesians 4:26–27). Anger nursed in the heart sours rapidly to hatred; for this reason it must be brought to the surface and acknowledged as soon as possible. Then a reconciliation can reasonably be sought, after which peace may be restored. If a reconciliation is impossible due to the impenitence of the other party, at least the basic issues will have been brought to the light of reason and one knows how to deal with the erring person in the future. What is brought into the open may not always attain healing, but at least it ceases to ferment in the unconscious and erupt periodically in words or actions of violence. We have to face the truth of the world's imperfection and our own part in it, that we too have sinned and fallen short of the glory of God within us. Jesus said on one famous occasion, "That one of you who is faultless shall throw the first stone", and the self-righteous throng of accusers of the adulterous woman quietly dispersed, until the woman and Christ were left alone together. He forgave her, but told her firmly not to sin again (John 7:53–8:11). It is of interest that the eldest accusers made their departure first: they had had more time for sinning than the younger members of the throng. These are usually the most dogmatic in the things of the Spirit because they are still so inexperienced as to believe that truth can be contained within rational categories, whether scientific or scriptural, to the exclusion of any deeper, emotional considerations. The greater truth of the Spirit is revealed to them as the experience of life chastens their self-esteem and brings them closer to the core of their identity.

This, of course, is where teachings of high spiritual charge have to be assimilated gradually; we can begin to make them our own only as we have climbed out of our own pit of darkness. When we hearken back to Somerset Maugham's fourth imaginary, but ever pertinent, temptation of Jesus by the devil, we can see that the danger of a religion of sacrifice is that its disciples can easily take the mantle of martyrdom from their Master without wearing it on their own shoulders. They suffer in their imagination the crucifixion of their Lord, the odium of which they then visit on all those who challenge their private beliefs. And so Christ is merely crucified again in the form of his people, who seek without ceasing the full impress of the truth. If the disciple dares to wear the Master's mantle, as Elisha did that of Elijah, he is changed spiritually, and then the imagination is firmly harnessed to the work at hand. He sees himself as a participant in the everlasting crucifixion of the God of truth, and then works in awe and humility for the coming of the Kingdom. No one is outside the bounds of that Kingdom, and the work of the disciple is to bring all around him to its awesome gates. According to his example they will either enter or remain outside: the final choice is theirs alone, but the manifest love of God in the faces of his servants can encourage the outsider to trust in a God of courtesy who does not override his creatures' will, but rather confirms and strengthens it.

The terror of unrestrained hatred is seen at its worst excesses in times of warfare. Each side is convinced that its interests are endangered by the other and that its own cause alone is the right one. In the Thirty Years War that ravaged Germany and the adjacent countries during the first half of the seventeenth century, the conflict was between Catholic and Protestant interests, but the result was a famine the like of which this part of the world had never previously experienced. The cruelty of many of the participants belied their Christian allegiance, unless, of course, we take to heart the terrible doctrine of the end justifying the means that came from the pen of a prince of the Catholic Church about a century before the Reformation. In much more recent times many of us have been witnesses of some of the barbarity of the Second World War. Few unbiased observers would disagree that the burden of atrocity was on the Nazi side – apart from its practice of genocide, it had no compunction in bombing defenceless populations alongside with, if not sometimes in preference to, genuine military targets. Since these unfortunate people did not belong to the "master race", it seemed not unreasonable to liquidate them indiscriminately!

But the fury soon spread to their allied antagonists. British aircraft played a vital part early on in defending their country against German invasion, and soon the military arm extended to attacking German supply depots and installations as well as essential power services. But the attacks did not end there. Round-the-clock bombing of saturation intensity left little of many German cities standing. It is only too natural that the delight of sheer destruction reinforced the zeal of the Allied bombing squads as they rained havoc on the civilians as well as the service staff of the hated enemy. This hatred was only too well merited in view of the enormity of the Hitlerite evil. But if one were to be honest about a matter that one can feel rather than judge impartially, there must have been a grim, impersonal satisfaction in seeing whole districts of major cities go up in smoke, the same type of enjoyment the Germans experienced earlier on in their wanton destruction of Rotterdam and Coventry. A vicious circle of virulent, destructive fury had been initiated, in which the main victims were helpless civilians who had played comparatively little part in the enormities of the Nazi programme. They had admittedly enjoyed its benefits at an earlier period, but were now to experience some of its less pleasant personal consequences in the tragedy of the death of loved ones and the destruction of homes and traditional landmarks.

It is evident that once a reign of violence is established, as in a situation of war, it will inevitably escalate by virtue of its own momentum. The human agent who initiated the violence soon becomes the prisoner of demonic forces far outside any rational control. These forces harness the human desire for revenge as well as pure delight in destruction, for it is so much easier and more satisfying to cast down than to raise up. Of course, the satisfaction of destruction is of limited duration, whereas the person involved in creative work has a much longer period of fulfilment to anticipate, but in the thrust of the moment in hand, the ejection of long pent-up emotions of disgust and hatred is orgiastic in intensity. Indeed, it can stimulate, or even replace, the orgasm of sexual union quite effectively in naturally sadistic people – and there are few of us completely free of sadistic tendencies, often, to be sure, concealed beneath a veneer of liberal tolerance or religious propriety. Once the lid is allowed off the emotional furnace, the steam scalds anyone in the vicinity, and the forces of darkness outside make common issue with the pandemonium within the psyche. Hell is indeed let loose, and its end is total destruction, with a return to the primal chaos from which the universe emerged by the divine fiat.

In any situation of popular disgust and violent rejection there are fortunately a few saner minds who can identify themselves with the hapless victims in the enemy camp. One such in Britain at the time of the Second World War was the saintly Bishop of Chichester, George Bell. Early on in the war he helped many Jewish refugees, who were interned because of their German origin and therefore stamped as possible agents of the enemy. Later on he was to protest against the indiscriminate bombing of German cities, with its toll of civilian casualties. His intervention was not popular with the sources of power, and he was labelled as pro-German by his antagonists. Indeed, his courageous stand almost certainly cost him translation to a more distinguished see, but he remained a witness to a higher ideal of humanity. He was a great friend of Dietrich Bonhoeffer, who gave up his life in trying to eliminate the demonic powers that held the German people in thrall, so that an honourable peace might yet be negotiated and the appalling carnage stopped. But at this stage a general madness was rampant: the Nazis would fight to the last drop of blood, while the Allied powers would be satisfied with nothing less than a total surrender of the fascist forces. It is, of course, easy with hindsight to shake one's head sadly at the pity of it all, but when one is in the thick of battle all sense of proportion is lost as the whole nation is enveloped in an enormous wave of inextinguishable fury that feeds hungrily on mass destruction and death. The hatred that the Nazis unleashed upon the Jews flowed back upon the German people with a terrible vengeance, which attained its peak at the wanton and completely ruthless destruction of the beautiful city of Dresden, crowded with refugees, at the end of the war.

While all this destruction was proceeding apace in Europe, tragedy enveloped the Far East also. The Japanese waged a war of horrible cruelty against the Chinese, with an insatiable lust for domination and expansion. It was inevitable that they should align themselves with the fascist powers of the west, and finally, in an act of monstrous treachery, they attacked and grievously maimed the United States' fleet at Pearl Harbour in Hawaii, while ostensibly engaged in negotiating a peace settlement. In the conflict against the Allied forces that followed, the Japanese captors treated their prisoners-of-war with a cruelty that knew nothing of the humane demands set by the Geneva Convention. In imperialistic Japanese eyes surrender was totally dishonourable, and so the unfortunate prisoners were regarded as lower than the vermin that stalked the empty streets. In due course the tide of fortune turned, and the once imperious Japanese, like their German allies, found themselves on the defensive and retreating fast. After the German capitulation in 1945 they continued the mad fight: it would have been an intolerable loss of face to surrender. The explosion of atomic bombs on Hiroshima and Nagasaki ended this display of vanity, but many thousands of helpless civilians died – and are still dying of the remote cancerous effects of ionizing radiation. That the bombing curtailed any further battle casualties is certain, but one can only weep at the mountains of dead noncombatants who, like the people in Jonah's Nineveh, could not tell their right hand from their left – speaking figuratively in terms of their ignorance of the imperialistic zeal that fired the war initially, to say nothing of the cruelty their armed forces had visited on other human beings helpless in their power as captives.

In this sad story too it is good to reflect on the witness of another Anglican bishop, Leonard Wilson of Singapore. He was humiliated and tortured by the Japanese when they captured that city. His face was so smashed that he was subsequently obliged to conceal the disfigurement under the cover of a beard, but his love and concern for his own flock overflowed to his torturers also. He never lost heart or succumbed to rancour. It was to be his privilege to baptize the soldier who had actually disfigured his face, and, as Bishop of Birmingham, his witness to the truth of the crucified, risen Lord never flagged. Indeed, the light shines in the darkness, which has never been able to extinguish it, try as it may. It is in the hearts of noble people that the Spirit of God reigns. From them a perpetual inspiration of light flows out to all their sleeping fellows at the foothills of Gethsemane. In due course the supreme test will be demanded of them also. Then they too will have graduated to the full stature of a human being.

It was the Russian people, however, who bore the full brunt of the German onslaught. Earlier on, the Russian government had made a pact with the Germans which involved the partition of Poland, a sad country that has seldom enjoyed freedom from the pressure or occupation of its two powerful neighbours. But when it suited Hitler's plans, the Russians were treacherously attacked, and appalling havoc was wrought on their vast country. Its grim survival was due not only to the unspeakable bravery and dedication of its people, but also to the severity of the winters and the "scorched-earth" policy which deprived the invaders of any provisions from captured territory. But then the tide turned, and the Soviet government gained control over the whole of eastern Europe in its constricting communist system, strangling every attempt at liberalization and freedom. The sad suppression of liberty in Hungary in the fifties, and Czechoslovakia in the sixties, is a dark indication of the powerful security demanded by a rigid dictatorial system, when tormented by memories of the past invasion and confronted by the present prosperity of its democratic neighbours. But the only true security comes from love, not arms. With love our neighbours are a very part of our own identity, not swallowed up, but free and contributing their own essence to the collective whole. This vision of heaven can, alas, never be attained by political or economic means, no matter how well-intentioned the systems may be. This is because their approach is essentially a cerebral one, but until the heart is changed from stone to flesh, the people will not respond in trust and self-giving service to the whole community of nations. The inner darkness controls the outer appearance, and the Antichrist is securely in control no matter how the system of government may style itself. He shows himself in the leaders of the enslaving nations, and projects himself into the minds of their adversaries.

It is clear that the forces of darkness thrive especially in situations of fear and confusion. They harness the traditional prejudices of the people so that the inner anger may erupt as destructive hatred. But even worse than hatred is cold indifference. Hatred does at least acknowledge the presence of the other person, even if that acknowledgement is passionately destructive. Indifference simply ignores the one it detests, and allows the natural process of attrition to do its lethal work. It is very doubtful whether the bulk of the German people had the faintest idea of what was happening in the concentration camps set up by the Nazi regime. Indeed, many probably did not even know of their existence. But the whole populace could witness the ostracism afforded their Jewish neighbours, the frequent attacks on their person by vicious thugs openly supported by the state, and the destruction of Jewish property, outrages which seemed to occasion no protest. Anyone actively succouring a Jewish victim would have incurred the displeasure of the civil authorities. But the inaction of the masses was clearly due to hostile indifference rather than to cringing servility. They were content to see this prosperous "alien" group reaping its wind of unpopularity. Yet in the end the "master race" reaped its own whirlwind of international opprobrium, as the country and people were systematically attacked and destroyed. All the Germans were losers, none with any cause for satisfaction, as the end of the Nazi regime drew near. Admittedly, the forces of fascist evil were defeated, but only at the expense of a partition of the country, with its eastern bloc heavily in bondage to Russian communism.

The old order is unceremoniously cast aside in the fury of discontent and hatred that accompanies war. But at least the place has been set for a new dispensation of power as the participants return once more to sanity and start to fashion a fresh life amid the rubble.

6

Powers and Principalities

St Paul, at the end of his letter to the Ephesians (6:10–20), speaks dramatically about the spiritual conflict that involves all living forms and especially the human being, who is God's messenger of light to the rest of creation. An angel is in fact a messenger, and we can act as good or bad angels according to our obedience to the Most High and our love of our neighbour, who is any creature near us. We read in the letter to the Ephesians:

Finally, then, put your strength in the Lord, in his mighty power. Put on all the armour which God provides, so that you may be able to stand firm against the devices of the devil. For our fight is not against human foes, but against cosmic powers, against the authorities and potentates of this dark world, against the superhuman forces of evil in the heavens.

The Authorized Version of the Bible translates the cosmic powers as "principalities and powers", which are enumerated theologically among the grades of the angelic hierarchy (in order of descending majesty there are seraphim, cherubim, thrones, dominations, principalities, powers, virtues, archangels and angels). Is St Paul's description of the ultimate sources of evil in the world merely a fiction based on the primitive psychology of his time, or is he speaking of objective entities that are in psychic contact with us through that "point" in the soul where we are able to communicate with intangible powers far beyond our normal consciousness?

The tendency in our "enlightened" century has been to demythologize the supra-rational aspect of the Bible, to relegate all accounts of inexplicable events to the realms of myth or illusion, so that human reason is the measure both of and for all things. Then we can be not only in charge of but also totally responsible for our lives on earth. This dogma concerning the intrapsychic origin of all unusual mental experiences certainly pleases both the psychologist and the social activist; the former does not need to concern himself about any focus of psychic activity outside the individual's mind, while the latter can attribute all unusual events to the unhealthy state of society. In this way the specialist in psychology and social studies can assume a complete oversight of the human condition. A belief in powers intermediate in situation between God and man can undeniably provide the ground for an abdication of the human will: we can then conveniently lay the burden of our own evil tendencies on demonic entities, and so evade personal responsibility for our actions and the subsequent course of our lives. The problem may be fascinating philosophically, but its importance is practical: is there an intermediate source of both good and evil that permeates the psychic dimension of communication and influences our actions? Neither biblical literalism nor critical demythologizing is an

adequate court of final appeal. As Jesus says to
Nicodemus in the course of their atmospheric nocturnal conversation, "In very truth I tell you we
speak of what we know, and testify to what we have
seen, and yet you all reject our testimony. If you
disbelieve me when I talk to you about things on
earth, how are you to believe if I should talk about
the things of heaven?" (John 3:11–12). In other
words, the matter is not so much one of debate as of
experience. But experience cannot simply be
accepted at its face value; it has then to be examined
scientifically according to the criteria of the accumulated wisdom of the ages, so that its significance may
be critically assessed. The ultimate criterion is the
integrity of the person and his mental balance,
remembering all the while that none of us is perfect
in either of these two respects.

We do well also to bear in mind the valuable
criterion of William of Occam, a Franciscan scholas-
tic philosopher of the fourteenth century. He is
known today especially for his saying, "It is vain to
do with more what can be done with fewer". This is
usually condensed in the famous maxim, "Entities
are not to be multiplied without necessity", which is
called Occam's razor. In the context of the present
consideration, do we really have to invoke the agency
of outer powers of darkness to explain, or at any rate
implement, the evil lying in the shadow of the
individual psyche? Cannot all the madness of the
world be contained within psychological and socio-
logical categories? Here we are wise to listen with
respect to those who have had experience of other
modalities of existence, but without accepting their
deductions uncritically. The psychic side of communication, from soul to soul without the intervention

of sensory information or rational deduction, is indeed hard to assess scientifically, because the information comes sporadically and usually wilts away if the faculty is challenged in a research laboratory. The scientific method demands that an experiment be repeatable in standard conditions. The hallmark of a scientific theory is that it is capable of being refuted. This is, as Karl Popper has shown, even more important than its verification. When we move into the study of psychic phenomena, their possible demonstration has then to be embraced in an over-all theory that demonstrates their significance in a living situation.

In my own life – and here it is more satisfactory to speak from personal experience rather than to hide behind vague generalizations based on data received from miscellaneous sources – I have been repeatedly aware of a realm or dimension of reality that has transcended but never occluded the material base of everyday existence. It has usually been of solemn hue (if one may be permitted to transcribe inner emotional impressions into the symbols of colour), but occasionally sharply accentuated around the atmosphere of certain individuals as a dark aura. I have known intuitively, even as a child, that such people were unwholesome – and sometimes a similarly unwholesome atmosphere has pervaded a house in which they lived or even had visited for a short time. In childhood I was aware of the terrible evil festering in Germany and the tortures committed on Jews and others detested by the Nazi regime. The pain was at times almost too severe to bear, but then an atmosphere of light penetrated the gloom, and the path of hope was shown again. Faith was the prerequisite for traversing that path when the radiance waned and I was on the solitary trail once more. In this gloom I was aware of presences whose origin I could not define. Some were probably the unquiet spirits of the dead, but a few had a darker, more forbidding emanation. These filled me with terror, but by holding fast to God, whom I had known from an amazingly early period of my childhood, I was supported and guided in this uncharted terrain of dark radiance. All this is, as already stated, an essentially private testimony, but the experience was to play an important part in my later work in the ministry of healing and deliverance, especially after I had submitted to the authority of the Church and received ordination as a priest. Priestly orders were to confer on me a spiritual authority that I lacked as a layman, even though I had been much involved in conducting retreats and in the ministry of counselling and healing for quite a number of years before I entered into the ordained ministry.

Almost at once, in my first parochial attachment, I was consulted by a man of artistic temperament but employed in the financial world, who had suffered from repeated bouts of severe depression which his doctors could only partially control with drugs. He came to me in a state of near-suicidal darkness, and suddenly I was aware of a malign presence overshadowing him. I asked him whether anyone close to him had recently died, and was told that, indeed, a colleague had just lost his life in distinctly unusual circumstances, so that suicide could not be excluded. This colleague had held a position of authority over the man, and had always behaved tyrannically towards him, making his life at work a constant misery. One would have expected his death to have come as something of a relief, but instead the depression intensified to near-suicidal proportions. There was certainly no question of grief for the dead man, nor any unresolved feeling of guilt about the unsatisfactory relationship in the past. It came upon me as a thundering shock that the dead man was obsessing (or infesting) the psyche of his sensitive colleague, with the intention of driving him also to suicide. The evil of the situation was overwhelming. I bade the "spirit" of the deceased one to depart forthwith into the protective custody of God, and at once the suicidal depression lifted from the sensitive man. He attained a balanced emotional frame very rapidly, and was able to leave the church in a state of calm relief. It later transpired that he was a natural sensitive, and he had to be instructed in the proper control of the psychic faculty. The depression, it must be admitted, did occasionally recur, but there was never again so terrible an episode that suicide was threatened. He was above all now in control of his life, and he subsequently left the world of finance for that of art.

This is a prototype example of the work that has subsequently been thrust upon me. I have been shown that bad relationships between parents and their children do not automatically terminate with the death of the former. On some occasions the "spirit" of the parent has hovered around the child's psyche and caused distress and even accidents, until once more the unquiet deceased were kindly, but with uncompromising authority, told to quit the earth-bound plane and move on to the greater life beyond death, to that place that God in his infinite mercy had prepared for their reception and healing. In some other instances, the disturbing entity has been a sibling or a more distant relative. Sometimes a sibling who has died in early childhood, even shortly after birth, has caused the disturbance. I would emphasize that this type of situation is not common, at least in my experience. I say this advisedly, lest a picture of the after-death state be painted in which all the recently deceased "spirits" hang around the living and cause unpleasant psychological disturbances. Fortunately, this is the exception rather than the rule: the penitent departed move to their apportioned place for further service and growth. We are accepted by God's grace, but we have to accept that grace whose full nature is love. It cannot be thrust upon us in such a way that our own inviolate will is outraged, a point not always appreciated by fervent revivalists who are hell-bent on saving the souls of all unbelievers. Yes, indeed, their heaven is too close to hell for the comfort of any perceptive individual, because the power of private judgement is overwhelmed in a seething emotional barrage of threats. The situation shades imperceptibly into the ways of the dictators of our time. In respect of the very young who have died and then obsessed the personalities of their siblings or other near relatives, their problem seems to be one of ignorance or else resentment that their lives have been cut short so summarily. In all these instances a Requiem Mass said for the dead can help to settle their souls, but often a word of command is also necessary. This has, indeed, been my experience.

All this is to be clearly distinguished from the practices of spiritualism. Here there is a willed attempt to communicate with the deceased through the agency of mediums, or sensitives. The impetus is nearly always the need of those who are bereaved or the curiosity of those dabbling in occult, potentially dangerous matters for the sake of new experiences. The results of this type of attempted contact are seldom satisfactory, since the issue is invariably clouded by the possibility of fraud on the part of the medium or else unconscious telepathic contact with the mind of the sitter. Even if what appears to be a genuine contact is made, the communication is very likely to be coloured by the personality of the medium. Furthermore, there is always the possibility of interference by mischievous entities from the vast intermediate psychic realm, some of which may well be of demonic nature. This is why willed communication by the agency of mediums is to be deprecated. But the phenomenon of mediumship is worthy of investigation by qualified research workers. These may, at the very least, gain new insights into the range of the human mind: the fruits of these studies are extensions of normal psychology (parapsychology). They shed new light on the mechanisms of life. Those who depend on communication through mediums with their dead loved ones tend to be drawn ineluctably into a prison of past associations which they then project into the present. Instead of growing through loss into a life of greater relationships with humanity at large, they remain stuck in past attitudes. By not letting go of the past, they remain trapped in it, and quite possibly restrict their loved ones on the other side of death.

The person who is naturally sensitive psychically is in possession of a gift that is both serviceable to others and wounding to himself. It must be used with reverence, and the call is from God, not man. If mediumship is indeed a valid means of communication with deceased souls, its purpose is to help those who are earth-bound on their journey to the light, and the operative work is prayer. It is conceivable that such entities are closer to the earth they once knew than to the "heavens" (using the term in a collective sense rather than one of spiritual distinction) they are to inhabit in their new form. And so their earthly helpers may assist the greater communion of saints in liberating them from past associations. Then the work is continued by that great communion, which surely includes the ministry of angels too. Such a sensitive person is, as I have already indicated from my own experience, vulnerable to the less desirable influences of the intermediate dimension (between solid earth and the heaven of the blessed departed), and needs constant protection. This is afforded by a life of humble submission to God in prayer, worship, service, and a chaste style of living. Furthermore, there should be unfailing prayer support from a devoted community: religious orders have an important place in this work, especially the contemplative communities whose life is centred on prayer. In this way the psychic faculty is sanctified. In the spiritualistic way it tends to be sensationalized, cheapened and brought into ridicule, at least among people with intelligence and spiritual discernment. All this is very sad, because the psychic mode is one of intimate communication between people and between the divine and the human.

On some occasions I have been aware of a powerful, more concentrated and malign source of disturbance around a person who is in severe difficulties. He may be aware of a destructive force around him that threatens his security, or there may be dangerous accidents, or simply an atmosphere of general disquiet. In these circumstances I have had little doubt that a demonic agency has been at work, rather than simply the unquiet soul of a deceased person. Sometimes the fallen angel, which is the usual identity of the demonic presence, has attached itself to a deceased person, so that the two appear to work in collaboration. Occasionally a decidedly evil deceased person may gain control over a neutral angelic presence on the lower grades of the hierarchy and use it for destructive purposes. All this, needless to say, is a purely private, subjective judgement which follows a personal encounter with a focus of evil. But the course of action is the same – to banish the entity, however it may be described, from the reaches of the earth and despatch it to the place in the greater world beyond death which God has prepared for it. It is essential to direct the demonic entity to a place of reception and not simply to leave it unattended in the darkness. Not only would this be very unloving, but it could also leave the entity free to continue its disturbing work among us all.

Some readers, disturbed enough by this account of obsessing demonic agents, would raise their eyebrows in incredulous horror at the suggestion of love being expended on such a vile entity. But we have, as Jesus once taught us, to love our enemies, and not only those who are well-disposed to us. Only the spirit of love can start the work of redemption. What God has in store for his errant creatures – remembering that he alone is the universal creator – is not our business, but it is surely not out of place to look for a final healing of all that is aberrant and unclean, whether human or angelic. Such must be the measure of divine love, of which human sacrificial love is a reflection in our little world. Such a universalistic hope does not in any way excuse, let alone overlook, the evil of the creature, which is to be expiated in full measure. But it can nevertheless envisage the sinner's final repentance, absolution and reception into the body of saints who are perpetually about their Father's business.

If we accept the thesis that there are agents of evil in the intermediate psychic realm, whether discarnate humans or fallen angels, can we postulate a personality of supreme evil, the devil? I believe we are entitled to do so, even if we cannot define the nature of the ultimate destructive power with precision. It may be a powerful fallen angel, or demon, or else the summation of all the evil power that has accumulated in the cosmos from the time of creation, especially since the Fall of the angels which was succeeded by the Fall of man in the mythological guise of Adam and Eve. Whatever may be the answer, it feels right to deal with the devil as a personal entity with whom we can attain a finite relationship, albeit a destructive one. This way seems better than being submerged in a vast ocean of darkness, floundering in dire panic. Since the devil strikes at the very root of the human personality, it seems not misguided to accept an element of the personal in its constitution. But more we cannot say. Personal experience often sheds light on dark areas of existence that far outdistance the dogmas of the rationalist.

A number of questions rise to mind. If there is indeed a vast nexus of cosmic evil (involving both the astronomical universe and the intermediate psychic realm), why does it appear to strike people so arbitrarily? The answer seems to lie in part in variations of individual sensitivity, especially where there is no protection by prayer in the lives of vulnerable people, like the man who was assailed by his dead colleague. Other people lay themselves open through unwise practices such as the use of the ouija board or their attendance at spiritualistic seances (these should be reserved for psychical research workers who know what they are doing, and certainly not be patronized by the general public). Again there are other people who, like Faust, deliberately give themselves over to the devil, just as spiritual aspirants dedicate their lives to God. Satanism itself is an evil cult that has always been part of the depraved mass of society, but is currently on the increase. Satanists believe that the Creator God has withdrawn from the world, never intervening any more in its affairs, and that the Son of God who has been given control of the earth in the Creator's absence is Satan, the god of this world (described in 2 Corinthians 4:4 as the god of this passing age). Jesus tried to destroy Satan's plan for the world, but it is, according to their belief, Satan that will attain the final victory. They participate in depraved rites and through psychic practices open themselves to the influence of satanic powers. The motives of its practitioners are mixed. Most are mentally or emotionally unbalanced, some are frankly evil people, while others get drawn into the scene as curious bystanders. These may later be the victims of blackmail.

I have no doubt that the practitioners of Satan worship are soon assaulted by evil forces, an infestation that shows itself in a progressive deterioration of the person's character. Deceitfulness, perverse sexual behaviour, stealing, and increasing destructiveness are typical features of this breakdown of the personality. To the rationalist all these changes can easily be attributed to fear and the general atmosphere of perversion that lies around zealous practitioners, but in practice there is usually a more concentrated focus of psychic assault in such cases, in addition to the psychological confusion that is drawn to the surface by the eruption of fear and hatred. It is certain that mentally balanced people do not espouse satanism, nor do they get involved in strange cults. It is the social misfit and emotional cripple who are attracted to bizarre activities of this kind. They are sad specimens of disordered humanity who seek power to affirm their shaky confidence. What they are really seeking is understanding and affection, but there are not many agencies who provide these needs, at least in a form that accepts the person as he is without imposing a rationalistic or a sectarian religious style of thinking upon him.

One thing is certain: the ministry of deliverance is both specialized and dangerous. It should not be embarked upon alone except in a situation of dire emergency. The ideal is collaboration on a professional level with other ministers of religion, specialists in psychological medicine, the social services, and, on occasion, the forces of law and order. Enthusiastic exorcists often do a great deal of harm because their zeal soon outdistances their powers of discernment. They tend to arouse considerable fear in the general public, and in the end bring the whole subject into disrepute.

Actual "possession" of a person by an alien force must be rare; I certainly have not encountered an instance, though I have met with people who have promptly attacked me physically when the word of deliverance was spoken over them. In my experience these people were always frauds, and had in due course to be confronted with their play-acting. On the other hand, a more distant influencing, called obsession or infestation, is not very uncommon. The entity causes distress, and sometimes appears to precipitate accidents or continual misfortunes. It can be removed by the word of command in the name of God the Holy Trinity, Father, Son and Holy Spirit. I prefer to do this work at a distance rather than in the person's presence; as I have already stated, most instances are due to the unquiet dead, but a number are demonic in quality and intensity of malice. On some occasions a place rather than a person is the seat of infestation. It too can usually be cleared at a distance, but sometimes it is necessary to work from within its precincts to complete the deliverance.

There are other possibilities that have to be considered. These include poltergeist activity, which is generally accepted as being due to misdirected psychic energy emitted by the client, nearly always an adolescent with sexual problems (though occasionally the subject may be much older), fraud, and mental disease which simulates the experience of possession. The usual cause is schizophrenia, a disease in which the patient often hears voices in his head which he may attribute to those of possessing entities within himself. There is also often a feeling of being influenced by outside forces or people; this may precipitate the delusion of being persecuted that is the basis of paranoia. Of course, it is not impossible that some schizophrenic subjects are abnormally sensitive psychically, and pick up other people's thoughts telepathically. But then their mental disturbance causes them to misinterpret what has been experienced, so that a gigantic conspiracy is conjured up in the imagination. The patient sees himself as the victim of slander and the object of unfair discrimination.

It is possible that the two men possessed of a legion of unclean spirits, whom Jesus exorcized at Gadara, were really schizophrenics, and the psychic disturbance that followed their sudden restoration to sanity affected a nearby herd of pigs so that they plunged precipitately into a lake and were drowned. The episode is recounted in Matthew 8:28–34 and with variations in Mark 5:1–20 and Luke 8:26–39. Certainly the incarceration of demonic entities in drowned animals would have been an unsatisfactory, if not a dangerous, way of disposing of them, for soon they would have broken free and caused even more trouble than before. We recall in this respect Jesus' teaching about an exorcized spirit roaming around in the wilderness, and then returning to its former home, only to find it more receptive than ever to re-infestation. And so the spirit returns with seven even more malicious spirits to its original abode (Matthew 12:43–45). Indeed, the last state of the victim is far worse than the first.

How does the sensitive person sense the "extrasensory", the psychic presence that seems to make so little impression on the great multitudes until its effect produces emotional reactions, some of which may be catastrophic? Usually one is aware of a source of information that enlightens the mind, as it did in the instance I described earlier on. Then one knows what one has to do, what is demanded of one. Very malign demonic forces hit one in the area of the solar plexus (the upper part of the abdomen) and induce a sensation of sickness. There is also a feeling of intense dread of panic proportions. One is empowered to lift all this up to God (praying in the top of the head), and then one is given the strength to proceed onwards with the work of deliverance. There are some evocative texts that seem to substantiate this upward raising of consciousness to God. "If I lift up my eyes to the hills, where shall I find help? Help comes only from the Lord, maker of heaven and earth" (Psalm 121:1–2). In the ethereal conversation between Nicodemus and Jesus in the secrecy of the night, Jesus says, "No one ever went up to heaven except the one who came down from heaven. The Son of Man must be lifted up as the serpent was lifted up by Moses in the wilderness, so that everyone who has faith in him may in him possess eternal life" (John 3:13–15). And finally we recall the crucifixion drama, "So they came to a place called Golgotha (which means 'Place of a skull'), and there he was offered a draught of wine mixed with gall . . ." (Matthew 27:33–54). To me these texts point to the high destiny of humanity: the scope of the intellect has to be extended by the intuition, and the whole is to be sanctified in the form of the crucified, resurrected Christ. What we know tremulously in the soul is ultimately to be realized boldly in the flesh, now made spiritual and therefore imperishable.

There are two extreme positions that would concur in dismissing, or at least violently repudiating, this exposition of psychic presence. One is atheistic and rationalistic, the other biblical and literalistic. The rationalist, applying Occam's razor with a vengeance, would place all paranormal experience without any further ado in the category of abnormal psychology – psychopathology in fact. According to this view all people claiming such insights have deluded minds, because the material world is alone real, and anything beyond its reach is pure illusion. Materialistic reductionism is certainly neat and tidy in its conclusions, but does it truly explain all the phenomena of life, to say nothing of personal inner experience? Since such a reductionism cannot be refuted, it fails to attain the distinction of a scientific theory; it remains a point of view, one of many in the constellation of metaphysical theories about the nature of reality. Because it appears to have a rational, scientific basis, it tends to exert undue influence on the untutored individual who holds science in great awe. To many people the detached, agnostic type of scientist is the ultimate purveyor of truth, and indeed, so he ought to be, but unfortunately his mind has its prejudices no less than the minds of naturally religious people. In other words, he too is a mere human being subject to our common frailties. When he speaks from the vantage-point of his own discipline he may well be an expert, but no one can be a master of all disciplines. Atheistic humanistic circles and those of religious triumphalism often share an unpleasantly strident arrogance that tends to silence all those with other opinions, so that, at least in the flurry of the current debate, they appear to have attained a victory. But the truth is greater than any human opinion; when we follow it we are led into many strange encounters that would have shocked us in the green period of our youthful assurance.

The biblical literalist has no difficulty in accepting the presence of the devil and his angels, so much so that, not infrequently, he sees an evil spirit lurking behind any situation of which he disapproves. It is the question of the unquiet dead that disturbs him, for the canonical Christian scriptures do not describe an intermediate state between the hell of the damned and the heaven of the saved. Therefore it seems clear that the evil ones are consigned eternally in hell, while the blessed live in heaven where there is eternal joy. According to the view of the believer, the judgement that precedes this final despatch may occur immediately after death, or else the deceased may rest in the earth where they have been laid, until the final, universal resurrection, which is contingent upon the coming in glory of Christ to judge both the living and the dead. But the outcome is the same: hell for the wicked and heaven for the blessed. Admittedly, the more catholic type of believer takes into consideration the teachings of the various books of the Apocrypha also. Prayer for the dead is commended in 2 Maccabees 12:41–45, a practice quite futile if the die had already been cast at the time of the person's decease: those in hell are outside the range of prayer, whereas the blessed in heaven do not need our prayers. Indeed, we need their concern day by day rather more than they ours!

It therefore follows, at least in the view of the biblical literalist, that the dead can neither communicate directly with us nor obsess a living person. All such phenomena are to him subtle impersonations by the devil, no doubt trying to delude us into believing that the souls of the departed are learning in a greater life beyond death. If every psychic phenomenon is dogmatically attributed to demonic interference, we once again find a view of reality that cannot be refuted, but neither can it be verified. In the end, those who have these experiences, or receive intimations of survival of loved ones in a greater framework of life, must come to their own conclusions. The phenomena may indeed be psychopathological hallucinations or demonic incursions. But they may also be genuine encounters on a psychic level far beyond intellectual analysis. The test is that of Jesus: you will recognize them by their fruits (Matthew 7:15–20), and the fruits are those of the Holy Spirit enumerated in Galatians 5:22, of which the first three are love, joy and peace. St Paul goes on to observe that there is no law dealing with such things as these. This criterion is the one that applies also to the ministry of deliverance. If the obsessed person (or locality) is freed of a psychic incubus, whether human or demonic, there is a change in the personality (or atmosphere) from fear to love, from foreboding to faith, from despair to hope. Of course, it could be that similar results might follow pure suggestion on the part of a therapist who had no special psychic sensitivity, but it is the duration of the relief that suggests the correct diagnosis. Some clients have already seen therapists without significant improvement, therefore pure suggestion seems an inadequate explanation for the sudden change that follows the work of deliverance. And here we have to rest in ignorance.

It seems to me that the writers of the Bible were much more perceptive spiritually than are we in our scientific age. On the other hand, we know very much more than they did about the world in which we live. The great advances in medical and psychological knowledge add a dimension to our understanding of human nature that Jesus himself lacked. To know all is indeed to forgive all, and God, who does have complete knowledge, is giving it ever more generously to his human children, provided they give of themselves to serve in love and not, as in the allegory of the Fall, merely seek after their own aggrandisement. The accounts of demon possession in the Gospels can now be subjected to Occam's razor more imaginatively. Thus the dumb man (Matthew 9:32–33), the man both dumb and blind (Matthew 12:22), and especially the boy afflicted with epilepsy (Mark 9:14–29) very probably did not have disorders caused by an evil spirit. Any such entity present would at most have aggravated them. We now know that epilepsy is due to a dysfunction of the brain: anticonvulsant drugs can abolish the fits but the basic tendency remains untouched. It may well be that a psychic influence sometimes acts as a trigger for the fits, but it would not be the fundamental cause of the trouble, which would remain located in the brain. If the boy was in fact permanently cured of his illness, Jesus must have effected a change in the brain far more significant than removing any outside influence that may have contributed to the trouble. Simple piety assumes that the cures Jesus effected were permanent, but no medical practitioner would be satisfied without a follow-up of many years. Indeed, complete healing far transcends the cure of a physical or mental ailment; it looks for the re-creation of the whole person in the image of God, of whom Jesus is our earthly exemplar. Until this ultimate healing has been attained, there is bound to be a recurrence of bodily troubles. Furthermore, this healing has communal as well as individual implications: full healing is no less than universal resurrection, and until this has been achieved, there will be relapses into disease no less than into national and international strife. The healings of Jesus are indications of the meaning of God's love for the individual. But the healed person is then expected to give what he has so marvellously received for the benefit of others. None of those whom Jesus healed rose to this height. Where were they when their Master was crucified?

This chapter has necessarily concentrated on the dark, forbidding aspects of the intermediate psychic dimension, but it should be remembered that there are also the blessed departed, now fully-fledged members of the Communion of Saints, as well as the angels of God's light. All help to bring the Spirit of God to our spirit, the holiest part of the soul where God is known because he dwells within us there. Were it not for the victory of light, the agents of darkness could never be discerned, let alone identified: a person in darkness is as helpless as if he were blind. All of us are open to this heavenly light provided we have the humility to watch, to listen and to pray.

7

The Divine Darkness

The darkness of God assumes a variety of appearances. To the mystic the darkness is a measure of the strength of God's light, uncreated and eternal, on the human soul. In much the same way as the direct impress of the sun on the naked eye would blind its sight by burning the retina, so the impingent rays of God's presence consume the secret place of the soul: a darkness heralds the divine splendour, the dazzling darkness of the mystic, which illuminates in its obscurity more than does the highest intellectual enlightenment. It is well said that no one can see God and remain alive. Job himself was treated to an account of the divine providence caring for the least of God's creatures as much as for the human with his immense intellectual grasp of the details of everyday life; the appearance of God out of the tempest was at once mitigated by the voice of wisdom to which Job could more easily attune himself. In the awesome account of Krishna's self-revelation to Arjuna in the eleventh chapter of the *Bhagavadgita*, the mighty warrior shrinks in terror at what he has been permitted to see. It is indeed a terrible thing to fall into the hands of the living God, especially if one has already apostasized from the divine allegiance (Hebrews

10:31), for the Lord is a devouring fire, described in Deuteronomy 4:24 also as a jealous God.

He is, however, also a God who is separate from all forms of thought. Possibly the greatest of the medieval Christian mystics, Meister Eckhart, says, "Why dost thou prate of God? Whatever thou sayest of him is untrue." St Augustine follows on, "There is in the mind no knowledge of God except the knowledge that it does not know him." He is the "Divine Dark" of Pseudo-Dionysius, and it is by "divine ignorance", or "unknowing", that the soul reaches the highest truth. The anonymous medieval author of *The Cloud of Unknowing* invokes the image of a cloud, in which all the normal mechanisms of the mind, such as imagination, perception and knowledge, are left behind. At the same time there is a "cloud of forgetting" as one enters the divine precincts. This is the same cloud that accompanied the Israelites each day on their journey from Egypt to the Promised Land, the cloud also that filled the Temple of Jerusalem when Isaiah was called to his prophetic ministry (Isaiah 6:1–9). Yet within this cloud there is greater illumination than in the mightiest seats of human knowledge, for one is free of all preconceptions and able to use the faculties of the soul without hindrance in a completely new way. And so, although no one has seen God, the truly illuminated person knows him by his emergent energies, uncreated inasmuch as they proceed directly from the Deity. The principal of these energies is love that brings all creatures into the freedom of service for the whole, and light that illuminates the reason with purpose, providing an insight into God's loving will, that the creature should participate in his very being (2 Peter 1:4).

There are instances, however, when both the love and the light appear to fail, and then the darkness is total; it is the result of a complete occlusion of light. While, as we read in Isaiah 45:19, God may speak with directness and clarity, and not secretly as in some corner of a darkened room, he still seems to hide himself quite often when we need him most. So it appeared to the fictional Job as he argued his case resolutely with his conventionally pious friends. It was much more frighteningly true of Jesus during the period of his passion, especially when he lay stretched out on the Cross and cried, "My God, my God, why hast thou forsaken me?" To many who cannot face this degree of dereliction in one who is God incarnate, the words are simply the first verse of Psalm 22, but their stark cry as recorded by St Matthew and St Mark points to a single utterance rather than a sequence in the repetition of a psalm. God is No-Thing, inasmuch as he cannot be likened to any created object, but at times he seems also to be Nothing, who can cause serious harm by inducing despair in those who have sought him in vain and officiousness in those who appoint themselves protectors of the injured person. Here is a darkness of existential magnitude rather than mystical quality.

But can the divine nature embrace a positive darkness, comparable with that of human nature, even the nature of wicked people? In our own time there have been outspoken voices that affirm the dark shadow in the Deity itself. Certainly the picture of God that emerges from the early part of the Old Testament is not one of reassuring compassion. From the destruction of the world at the time of Noah to the obliteration of the cities of Sodom and Gomorrah later on, the wrath of God dominates the scene. The destruction of the Egyptian people at the time of Moses confirms this tendency – indeed, God is portrayed as knowing the intentions deep in the heart of Pharaoh so as to decree in advance the plagues that are to destroy his country. And so God wins glory for himself at the expense of the Egyptians. He cares tenderly for his chosen people Israel, providing they behave themselves dutifully during the journey of the Exodus, but punishes any insubordination with a terrible severity that occasions the death of many people. Joshua too, when he crosses the Jordan into Palestine, is told to raze the cities of Jericho and Ai to the ground when their inhabitants stand in the way of the colonization of the country by God's chosen ones. In 2 Samuel 24 we read of God's terrible anger against David and his people after David has been tempted into making a census of the people of Israel and Judah: a pestilence lasting three days is decreed in which seventy thousand people die. It is of interest in this account that God is identified as both the tempter and the executor of the sentence, and his wrath is assuaged only by David buying the threshing-floor of an alien, building an altar on it and sacrificing abundantly to God. In the parallel account in 1 Chronicles 21, which was written some centuries later, it is Satan who is identified as the tempter. When we consider the strange episode, almost of nightmare intensity, of Jacob's struggle with the angel of God in the middle of the night, the heavenly antagonist seems to be as close to Satan as to God.

Jacob survives the attack and demands a blessing from his celestial visitor, who changes his name (and therefore the quality of his renewed nature) to Israel, which means one who has been strong against God and who in turn is a champion of God. Whatever we may make of all these accounts, there is little doubt that a dark shadow side of God is revealed, one that terrifies in its brutal mastery but shows little compassion to anyone who opposes its will.

Perhaps the best known book that emphasizes God's moral ambiguity is Carl G. Jung's *Answer to Job*. In this speculation, Jung sees Job's terrible afflictions as a manifestation of the divine cruelty exerted on a human being who is apparently more spiritually sensitive than God himself. Indeed, according to this controversial argument, God is forced to meet and accept his own shadow side in this encounter, and then he seeks incarnation in human form in order to come to terms with it and ultimately overcome it. The supreme incarnation is that of Jesus, in whom God achieves the goal; now at last he has succeeded in transcending his shadow side. Therefore we may say that if the light of God is uncreated light and unfailing love, his shadow, which is involved in the life on earth, is heartless cruelty. God seeks perpetual incarnation in the human soul for the union of his opposite tendencies, and in Christ the resolution of the antinomy has been achieved. Such a God would scarcely evoke a loving worship, however, even if naked fear might keep his creatures obedient to his inscrutable vagaries. Nevertheless, monotheism does affirm that God is the creator of light and darkness, author alike of prosperity and trouble (Isaiah 45:7). There is no god beside him, who puts to death and keeps alive, who both wounds and heals (Deuteronomy 32:39). Whatever repugnance we may feel against a God who sends forth pain and suffering by his creative word no less than light and vibrant life in his eternal mode, we gladly give thanks that he is in ultimate charge of the cosmos, mysterious as his ways must appear to us as we plod on day by day with vision restricted to our immediate task.

It is apparent that there is still no satisfactory philosophical solution to the paradox of rampant evil and chaos in a universe created and governed by a loving, all-powerful God. It is apparent also that the human mind cannot avoid the tendency of making a god in man's image, even though we believe that God fashioned us in his own image. This "anthropomorphism" may be simplistic to the point of naïvety, but it need not be disdained. "If a man says, 'I love God', while hating his brother, he is a liar. If he does not love the brother whom he has seen, it cannot be that he loves God whom he has not seen" (1 John 4:19–20). God shows himself to us in the form of human experience, and our understanding of him is closely related to our innate temperament. Oskar Pfister, a Swiss Lutheran pastor and disciple of Freud (even though he could not accept the dogmatic atheism of the great man), said, "Tell me what you find in the Bible, and I will tell you what sort of a person you are." It is noteworthy that as the pages of the Old Testament unfold, so does a kinder, more loving God emerge, beautifully portrayed in Psalm 103, "The Lord is compassionate and gracious, long-suffering and for ever constant; he will not always be the accuser or nurse his anger for all time. He has not treated us as our sins deserve or requited us for our misdeeds" (vv. 8–10). The same loving God suffering agonies over his unfaithful spouse, his ungrateful child Israel, is portrayed in the moving prophecy of Hosea. Punishment follows sinfulness, but God is more than ready to take the initiative in restoring relationships once there has been even a flicker of repentance. In Isaiah 53 the face of God is revealed in the sacrifice of the Suffering Servant, by whose scourging the world is healed, a picture perhaps of the prophet Jeremiah, but made fully real in the person of Jesus who is at once the man for others and the Word of God made flesh.

But even the gospels portray a God of vengeance no less than one of love, and his wrath, at least in some of the more terrifying parables, like that of the Sheep and the Goats (Matthew 25:31–46), knows no ending for those who have done wrong and not repented at the end of this short life on earth. Nevertheless, the theme of God's love does predominate in the New Testament, shown in the free sacrifice of Jesus for the reconciliation of the world to God, and brought down to earth in an intelligible context in St Paul's radiant outpouring in 1 Corinthians 13, as well as in the parables of Luke 15:1–32: the Lost Sheep, the Lost Coin, and especially the Prodigal Son. Somehow a balance has to be struck between an affectionate acceptance that sweeps aside all past misdemeanours, and a judgemental wrath that condemns a large body of mankind to eternal damnation. The first can become permissive to the point of moral indifference, the second so frightening that the individual is coerced into righteousness in the fear of perpetual exclusion from the presence of God. Such a righteousness, as we have already seen, can lead to an egoistic virtuousness, typical of the Pharisee in the famous parable, that is completely devoid of love. The end is a persecution of all foreign elements who threaten the precarious faith of the believer.

Authentic love accepts a person for what he is now in order to direct him to what he is to become – a true son of God modelled on the figure of Christ but within the integrity of his own personality. The famous words of Galatians 2:19 sum this up well, "I have been crucified with Christ: the life I now live is not my life, but the life which Christ lives in me." If acceptance brings the person to the valley of decision, the urgency of the situation makes him dedicate himself at once to God rather than remaining in a state of uncommitted agnosticism. Acceptance should be lovingly infused with urgency, since the present moment is of vital importance in a person's later development. But the end is not a promise of future heavenly favours so much as a present experience of freedom in the service of God and the creation around us. This freedom is eternal, heavenly bliss, and it looks for nothing beyond itself. Furthermore, as we now are, so we shall continue in the future, whether here or in the life beyond death. It is in this frame of mind that the pure love of God is known without any menacing shadow to distort it. Needless to say, the attainment of this blessed state of equanimity is a product of divine grace on the one hand and human toil in service and daily sacrifice on the other. If the attainment is selfishly contrived, the ego interposes itself between God and the person; all his endeavours fail, and he moves into the darkness of isolation until he has learned the lesson of humility.

With all these considerations in mind I personally

do not accept a fundamental shadow side of God. The creative principle of the universe, called the Godhead, is beyond the dualities of human conception – indeed the divine darkness, the cloud that fills us with divine ignorance. This immeasurable, ineffable being manifests itself in the universe as a tangible presence whom we can know and worship in love and dedication of ourselves to the highest we may conceive. This is the personal God whose effulgence of love sustains the universe. In Hindu thought the ineffable Brahma shows itself in the world as the personal Isvara, which is responsible for the creation, preservation and dissolution of the universe. The Supreme therefore has two natures, the higher, which is incomprehensible, and the lower, which is the object of worship, whose very nature is love. In the words of Jakob Boehme, "Creation was the act of the Father; the incarnation that of the Son, while the end of the world will be brought about through the operation of the Holy Spirit." They are all one God, and each fulfils every function, but each one has a pre-eminence, according to his nature, over the others. The end of the world is to be seen as the dissolution of present forms in preparation for a glory as yet unrevealed except in mystical illumination. And yet that glory was there at the beginning, it is now, and it shall always be in a created order that has no end other than in the mind of God. The process of creation seems to be a gift of pure divine grace so that innumerable forms might enjoy finite existence. The end of the purpose of creation is the raising up of all those forms to the divine light, in whose loving radiance they are transfigured, dissolved, and finally resurrected in the uncreated energies of God.

This God, the living image of the incomprehensible Godhead, is pure light and unceasing love. In the words of 1 John 1:5, God is light and in him there is no darkness at all. It is we who are dazzled by the intensity of the light into the darkness of silence, in the hush of which the light penetrates the inner depths of the psyche, revealing everything that was hidden, unwholesome and sinful. In that light we start to see ourselves unshielded by any illusions; the darkness within is illuminated so that its composite elements are brought to our knowledge. The love that accompanies the light works towards their integration and the healing of the personality. Dame Julian of Norwich saw truly: "I saw no wrath but on man's part; and that forgiveth he in us. For wrath is not else but a frowardness and a contrariness to peace and love and either it cometh of failing of might, or of failing of wisdom, or of failing of goodness: which failing is not in God but is on our part" (Chapter 98 of *Revelations of Divine Love*). William Law also, some three hundred and fifty years later, came to a similar conclusion in his last writings, *The Spirit of Prayer* and *The Spirit of Love*. God's will is restoration, not rejection, but we must remember that love remains inactive until it is accepted by the beloved, and the gift of free will determines this acceptance. God himself cannot force his attentions on his creatures without annulling the freedom of choice he has given them. Here lies the impasse, the tragedy of creation.

To me, the apparent wrath of God is embodied in the law by which the universe is governed no less than our lives on earth. Psalm 19 juxtaposes the cosmic law very effectively with the law that God gave to his chosen people, and through them to mankind as a whole, by the prophetic word of Moses. "The heavens tell out the glory of God, the vault of heaven reveals his handiwork . . . The law of the Lord is perfect and revives the soul. The Lord's instruction never fails, and makes the simple wise." If we live within the compass of that law, we shall be safe, but if we disregard it, we shall suffer. Much of the Wisdom literature of the Bible, especially the Book of Proverbs, amplifies this theme, which, within its limits, contains much truth. Those who lead chaste, sober, disciplined lives are certainly less liable to disease and misfortune than those who cannot curb their appetites and lusts. But the case is less clear-cut than this: the story of Job's sufferings demolishes a comfortable theory of simple cause and effect, for here a perfectly righteous man suffers abominably, and he, to his credit, does not flinch from asserting his innocence, even at the cost of setting himself up against God, whose favour he might have curried by an attitude of obsequious self-denigration. One's mind harks back to the absurdity of the confessions of treason exacted from Stalin's antagonists in the infamous Moscow trials of the late thirties. Job, being of an infinitely stronger moral fibre than those ambivalent victims of injustice, does not betray the truth.

The story of Job is repeated with inevitable personal variations in the lives of the world's martyrs, not only those who adorn the official hagiography (the biographies of the great saints of the religious traditions), but also the ordinary folk who suffer

terrible misfortune of a degree quite out of proportion to their failings as people. One thinks of the
young victims of progressive crippling disease,
cancer and mental breakdown, and the older ones
whose lives are brought low by senile dementia, to
say nothing of the countless multitudes who have
died in prison camps and in the wake of nuclear fall-
out. Nevertheless, before we cringe at the arbitrary
wrath of an inscrutable God, we should remember
that we do not live private lives in isolation from the
greater community. We are, on the contrary, all parts
of the one body. This famous statement of Ephesians
4:25 may have applied especially to the members of
the young Christian community, but it is also true of
humanity as a whole. The purpose of a spiritually
orientated group is not simply one of mutual support, which, of course, is fundamental, but also one
of service to all people, the whole created universe in
so far as this impinges on it. The supreme action is
prayer, for in it the power of God infuses the person
with a greater potential for service consequent on his
inner renewal than would be possible if he simply
relied on his own strength.

Membership of the human race brings with it the
advantages of civilization which we tend to take for
granted until they are taken away from us. But we
are also exposed to the communal, indeed global,
sinfulness of man, so that even if our own lives have
been relatively blameless, we are called on, in the
likeness of Christ, to assume some of the many
burdens of the less perfect members of society around
us. Suffering, in other words, is essentially retribu-
tive for those on the lower rungs of the spiritual
ladder. As we ascend painfully to the enlightenment

that finds its apogee in love, so our suffering assumes a redemptive quality both for ourselves and the greater body of creation around us. We remember St Paul's famous insight here, that although the whole created universe groans in all its parts as if in the pangs of childbirth, it is to be freed from the shackles of mortality and to enter upon the liberty and splendour of the children of God (Romans 8:21–22). This, I believe, is the great purpose and destiny ahead of the human race, but first of all it has to get its own house in order. The winnowing effect of suffering shrives it of illusions of grandeur, ownership and complete autonomy. Then alone may humility leave it open to the creative power of God, who is eternally making all things new (in the vision of Revelation 21:5).

But how does the suffering arise? In the allegory of the creation and the fall, while Adam and Eve are in heaven they live in a child's world, ignorant both of God and of their own identity. When they yield to the temptation of satisfying themselves in disobedience to God's strict instruction, they at once fall from their innocent state of ignorant bliss and enter upon an adult world of separation and suffering. Now at last they know God in their distance from him, just as they know themselves in their separate identity. The great work is one of returning to God in corporate unity as responsible adults, who can contribute their individual talents to the communal welfare, and not simply thrive on it like thoughtless children. "The tempter, the serpent, was more crafty than any wild creature that the Lord God had made" (Genesis 3:1). It is evident that God has made provision for evil in the universe no less than for good.

Whether the evil is a primary quality of the creation or a secondary consequence of the ignorant, self-centred response of the disobedient creature we cannot tell – in fact, the two possibilities merge when we ponder the matter deeply. It seems clear to me that this was part of the divine plan, for without the constant threat of extinction there would be no mental development. Sin is indeed a necessary part of life, as Julian of Norwich was told, but nevertheless in the end all shall be well. Sin plays a needful part in bringing us to the depths of our own being, so that, when its consequences are faced, we may seek divine forgiveness. And so love enters the heart, a love from God that enables us to love ourselves in all our frailty and then to love our fellow creatures in their frailty also. It is no mystery that the repentant sinners in Jesus' parables, and also in the course of his daily ministry, are much closer to God than are their cold, virtuous detractors. These latter live to the letter of the law, but the spirit underlying it is far beyond their comprehension. That spirit is love, a gift of God which cannot be induced, let alone contrived, by the human soul acting alone. The essence of that love is a constant giving of oneself to God's care day by day, in all one's frailties, not a striving for personal mastery that puts oneself far above others in one's excellence.

When we can accept the manifest presence of evil in the creative process, interestingly we become less dominated by its power. By coming to terms with the springs of evil in the world no less than deep within ourselves, we are in a stronger position to master it, so that its dynamic potential can be deflected and neutralized. It is precisely those who

are most fearful of evil, striving obsessively to eliminate it according to their own insights, that are
specially vulnerable to its naked, demonic thrust.
They are tempted to project it on to those whom
they personally dislike. On the other hand, we dare
not trifle with evil, let alone tolerate its effects in our
midst. It may be the destructive impetus without
which conscious growth would soon come to an
end, but left unchecked it would soon cast the
creation back to the primary chaos out of which the
cosmos evolved. It is in this context that we can
begin to grasp Christ's injunction against resisting
evil: the more it is hated, the more does it thrive on
that hatred. But if it is accepted and sent back in love
to God, from whom it too finds its challenging
origin and final consummation, a blessing may
remain for all involved in the transaction, not exclud-
ing the evil thing itself. "You have learned that they
were told, 'Eye for eye, tooth for tooth'. But what I
tell you is this: Do not set yourself against the man
who wrongs you. If someone slaps you on the right
cheek, turn and offer him your left" (Matthew
5:38–39). The problem is, of course, how to put this
injunction into practice, when there is a seething
ferment of anger within oneself. Once we can accept
the dark side of reality as a fact within our own
psyche no less than in that of other people, we can
be still and carry out the sacred act of compassion
even when anger gnaws at the root of our being. As
the action of reconciliation is repeated, so will the
resentment deep in the heart be mollified until, with
the passage of time, it is imperceptible save for the
awareness of a quiet forgiveness that shows itself in a
greater love for those around one. But forgiveness

does not annul truth; those who have acted dishonestly have to face their own corruption before they can be healed. The measure of this healing is their will to restore the damage they have done.

In fact, the inner mechanism of this slow change of heart to forgiveness is the presence of the Holy Spirit deep within the soul. Usually our emotions take us over so precipitately and with such overwhelming power that the inner light is eclipsed by the darkness of personal grievance. But if we can learn to be quiet, the voice of God can still be heard, and the inner power that radiates from that voice can strengthen us in the way of forbearance, even when the world itself seems to be falling in pieces around us: "Be still, and know that I am God" (Psalm 46:10). This psalm reminds us that, no matter how menacing the outer situation may be, God is still in charge of events: If we remain calm in prayer, we will know the divine presence within us, no less than in the outer turmoil. And then we can act as responsible human beings, infused with the power of God. This seems to be the usual effect of prayer: the problem is not so much solved from without as we are strengthened within so that we may learn to cope more responsibly with it. Most problems remain insoluble until people grow into something of the stature of Christ himself, or as Jesus would have put it: for mankind it is impossible, but all things are possible for God.

There is, however, a time when God's presence does seem to fade from our sight. We have already considered the existential darkness which follows the apparent withdrawal of God from our lives. It happened to the fictional Job, and all his debates with his three friends ended in a silence of ignorance. It happened to Christ on the cross when he cried out in despair to the God who had forsaken him; he received no reply except the taunts of the onlookers. It happened to the victims of the Holocaust in Europe no less than to those on whom the atomic bomb fell in Japan. It happens day by day to those who are afflicted with terrible diseases that yield neither to medical treatment nor to prayer. Where was God then? How could a God of love tolerate such enormities, whether of existence itself or of the evil that people inflict on each other? Surely he could have intervened! This is the ultimate problem confronting all who believe in divine providence, who worship a God of love. The solution to this problem, as far as I am permitted to see, is that the victim is being prepared for growth into the stature of a full person, no less than Christ himself. Certainly the God who showed himself to Job did not reveal the nature of the contest he and Satan were having at Job's expense, but Job grew sufficiently through his trials, bravely if rebelliously borne, to see God directly. The God he had worshipped from afar, sincerely enough but with an undercurrent of fear lest misfortune should strike his family, had now disclosed himself as a living presence whom Job could know personally. All his suffering faded away as a triviality in the face of this supreme revelation, and we may be sure that Job's attitude to possessions and human relationships was far less clinging after that encounter.

In the same way the crucifixion drama, an event of terrible failure in the perspective of Good Friday, found its consummation in the Resurrection two days later. But neither Job nor Jesus could glimpse the victory in the darkness of the hell they were obliged to experience.

> In the days of his earthly life he offered up prayers and supplications, with loud cries and tears, to God who was able to deliver him from the grave. Because of his humble submission his prayer was heard: son though he was, he learned obedience in the school of suffering, and once perfected became the source of eternal salvation for all who obey him, named by God high priest in the succession of Melchizedek (Hebrews 5:7–10).

One might add, in response to this famous passage, that Jesus' prayers were not apparently heard either in Gethsemane or on the cross at Calvary. Jesus had to do the great work of reconciling the world to God on his own, while the Father stood by in his own helpless grief. It was his previous prayer life that sustained Jesus in this period of darkness, when prayer, indeed faith itself, seemed a pitiful delusion. But he persevered in the darkness and he attained the victory over the forces of evil, so that the Father could declare him Son of God by a mighty act in that he rose from the dead (Romans 1:4). The God who lamented so sadly the idolatries of faithless Israel in the prophecy of Hosea, wept even more at the suffering of Jesus. And this lament has continued; Christ will indeed be in agony until the end of the world, as Pascal said. In the pain of his creatures, their disease and their cruelty to each other, God suffers, but he may not intervene until they too have attained their own blessing, as did Jacob when he wrestled with the angel of God in the darkness of a lonely night fraught with foreboding but consummated in victory. This is the purpose of incarnation, whether divine or human.

To see what this means on an earthly level we need only meditate upon the father of the Prodigal Son. He did not interfere when the thoughtless boy took the money due to him, and went out into the world squandering all he had on vice. The father could never, we may be sure, take his mind off his ungrateful son, praying for him constantly, but being quite unable to assist him in his travail. When the boy was in destitution he could at last, in the silence, come to himself and yearn sincerely for his father's support. Only then could the father run out to meet the stricken boy, not with recriminations but in paeans of joy. The son could, however, have remained obdurate, in which case the father's love, though never ceasing, would have been powerless. We can only hope that all sentient life will eventually respond to the love of God and move towards its own way of resurrection. This is the way in which the evil, separative impulse is redeemed and healed. But until there is this universal response to God's love, the innocent will suffer as they take on the burden of their sinful brethren. They too will, however unconsciously, assume the role of the Suffering Servant, by whose scourging healing comes to the world. In this life their end, like that of Jesus, may be appalling, but there is much experience of God's love ahead of them. To grow progressively into the knowledge of God is the end of the spiritual quest.

8

Can These Bones Live?

This rhetorical question was put to Ezekiel by God, who carried him away by the Holy Spirit and laid him down in the middle of a valley full of bones. Ezekiel deferred the answer to God, who bade him prophesy over the bones. Life was infused into them, flesh with its sinews and skin covered them, and they arose as a great army. This vision was enacted as a symbol of the restoration of the whole House of Israel from the captivity in Babylon, where a hopeless resignation reigned, to the Holy Land, where they were to return and rebuild the Temple of Jerusalem and the walls of the city (Ezekiel 37:1–14). This remarkable vision of resurrection was to presage the return in strength of the Jews to their homeland after about seventy years' exile. It also points to the resurrection of the chastened individual to a heightened awareness, whether in this life or the greater life beyond mortal death. Nothing remains static in the world of God, for he is a Living God, sharing in the experience of his creatures as they enter a fuller existence of personal growth and actualization.

When the Word became flesh and dwelt among us, not only did he impart invaluable teaching to mankind, but he also learned what it was to be human, to know the frustrating impotence of an intelligence of vibrant creativity incarcerated in an animal body. As St Paul writes, "If you are guided by the Spirit you will not fulfil the desires of your lower nature. That nature sets its desires against the Spirit, while the Spirit fights against it" (Galatians 5:16–17). In Christ, who is the eternal new man, the spirit inhabits the flesh so as to bring it to a spiritual resurrection, as manifested in the resurrection body of Jesus himself. In this way the conflict so apparent in the lives of us all is resolved not in a categorical unilateral victory but in a growth in understanding of both parties. The flesh is raised beyond selfish desire to spiritual consciousness, while the Spirit, by its incarnation, learns compassion. How easy and satisfying it is to judge and condemn those who have personality difficulties that shut them off from the community! How much more illuminating and humbling it is to experience a particular difficulty oneself! Then at last do judgement and condemnation of people, both forbidden by Christ, broaden into understanding and compassion. I do not find it unseemly to reflect on God himself learning compassion through the process of incarnation. As we learn by his presence within us, so he learns by that presence also. "The eye with which I see God is the same with which God sees me", said Meister Eckhart. It is through his presence in all things that he knows the meanest creature as intimately as he does the most brilliant. "Are not sparrows two a penny? Yet without your Father's leave not one of them can fall to the ground. As for you, even the hairs of your head have been counted. So have no fear; you are worth more than any number of sparrows" (Matthew

10:29–31). This statement is not pantheism, the identification of God with the universe, but rather panentheism, an affirmation of the divine presence in all that is made. The Creator is separate from his creation while at the same time intimately involved in its welfare moment by moment.

This is the essence of God's love, and the basis of our hope that the creation may, in a time beyond time, move beyond death to the splendour of the liberty of God's children, to quote Romans 8:21 once again. Then at last the will of the creature may be so chastened, resurrected and glorified that it can work constructively with the will of God. God is neither a remote potentate so detached from his creation that he lets it proceed with its own destiny without any further concern, nor is he an obsessively interfering parent who cannot bear his children to get on with their own lives. His joy is greatest once we have attained to that degree of responsibility when we can order our lives and the government of the world aright, without the necessity of constantly calling on him for emergency assistance. But in the meantime he is available in urgent shafts of prayer. When the consummation of all things comes, there will be an awareness of the constant presence of God in our lives, so that the sacred and the profane shall be one. And so we can say, "Here and now, dear friends, we are God's children; what we shall be has not yet been disclosed, but we know that when it is disclosed, we shall be like him, because we shall see him as he is" (1 John 3:2). It is this hope that leads us to purify ourselves, as Christ is pure. The essential prerequisite is humility.

When we reflect on the events of the last part of

our century in the light of the resurrection prophesied by Ezekiel, some interesting conclusions strike home. Even though the imperialistic Japanese rained havoc on south-east Asia, their victories burst the bubble of European supremacy: within two decades virtually all the outposts of western colonial rule had fallen, although the heritage of its civilization continues to survive in the emancipated countries side by side with their native culture. The same is largely true of the African continent, except in South Africa, where there is an ongoing battle between a powerful, now indigenous, white minority striving desperately to preserve its ascendancy, and an oppressed black majority, striving equally hard for its liberation from the cruel, unjust "apartheid" system that has gained the government of the country international opprobrium. Each group is seeking its preservation, but only a few can see how the one is intimately dependent on the other for a full individual identity. We are indeed all parts of the one body, and our integrity depends on the health of that body quite as much as on our own qualities.

It is ironical to find that Germany and Japan, only a short while ago so eager for world conquest, are now the bastions of the western monetary system – this applies, of course, to the Federal Republic of Germany and not the German Democratic Republic, which is firmly anchored to the Russian communist bloc and infinitely poorer as a consequence. The determined industry of the Germans and Japanese, together with their high intelligence, have led to this new phase of development. Money has apparently proved a very acceptable substitute for military power – both countries were heavily punished for their aggressiveness – and is certainly safer, even if its influence does not have a noticeably more spiritual impact.

The field of world religion has also shown dramatic changes. The Jews, the very subject of Ezekiel's vision 2,600 years ago, have indeed been resurrected into a new people. Apart from the Israelis' military strength and emotional toughness, the wider Jewish community is now resolute, confident and self-affirming; though anti-Judaism is still a force in the world, the somewhat cringing attitude the Jews had to their neighbours is now a thing of the past, and they are proud of their identity. The enormity of the Holocaust has certainly cleared their collective unconscious of any lingering guilt concerning their ancestors' part in the death of Jesus. Their alleged cry to Pilate, when they chose Bar-Abbas for release and Jesus for death, "His blood be on us, and on our children" (Matthew 27:26), has been fully expiated by their descendants' suffering. It is rather to the compliant Christian clergy in Nazi Germany that the stigma of guilt now attaches, a stigma that has cut down to size the erstwhile triumphalistic assurance of the Christian Church. But a wiser, less inflated Church is now much closer to the underprivileged, the downtrodden, and the politically oppressed. The prophets of Israel are no doubt sighing with relief at this transformation from their heavenly vantage ground!

In much of western Europe the people are largely ignorant of their Christian heritage, and the Church appears more like a missionary outpost than a bastion of spiritual identity. This in itself is not necessarily to be deplored, for those who now worship do so out of conviction and not compliant conformity. The resurgence of the Russian Orthodox Church is a case in point. Thrown ignominiously out of power by the communist regime, it has learnt humility both at home and in the west; its deeply spiritual roots and magnificent liturgy have won for it a significant number of converts among a questing population left unfulfilled by its native faith.

There has been a great outburst of ecumenical collaboration amongst the various Christian denominations in recent years. A most important turning-point was the love of Pope John XXIII. His inspiration in convening the Second Vatican Council, despite much discouragement from those closest to him, summoned the most powerful of all the Christian communions, the Roman Catholic, out of the darkness of self-assured triumphalism into the light of questing openness to the present world with its burning incentive to human collaboration. But it must be admitted that the ecumenical movement speaks only to a minority of the population of nominally Christian countries; while it arouses considerable general interest, as do the pronouncements of various church leaders, its impact on the spiritual life of the masses is slight. And yet there is a deep yearning for illumination amongst many intelligent people who have found little inspiration in the traditional communions. The immigration of various Asian groups to Europe has led to the implantation of large Muslim, Hindu, Sikh and Buddhist communities in a society that was once solidly Christian with a modest admixture of Jews, who were cautioned to discreet silence in the face of general mistrust and ignorance. These Asian groups not only observe their own faiths far more zealously than do most nominal Christians, but have also contributed their quota of spiritual understanding to younger generations who are seeking more immediate religious experience and less traditional dogma. Certainly the current interest in meditation and prayer owes a considerable debt to the example and practice of Sufi, Hindu and Buddhist masters.

It is not uncommon for young, well-educated westerners to jettison their Christian faith and embark on the Asian journey to liberation and enlightenment. Some live for a considerable time in a Hindu ashram or attached to a Buddhist vihara, either locally or in an Asian country. But then comes a yearning for return. The spirit of Christ in their traditional background beckons many back home, and they return to the Christian fold with an understanding of a completely different order to that with which they had originally left. It is the Catholic tradition that receives most of these home-comers, who then discover that all they had learned was already available in the Christian way, though it had somehow been overlaid by a formalism that had almost obliterated the traces of its spirituality.

It needs also to be said that not all practitioners of the wisdom of the east are holy people. Charlatans abound, and there are also powerful psychic currents of great destructiveness in a very mixed religious milieu. But then the same is true of the western religious traditions, even though the evil may be more subtly masked and plausibly contained in imposing ecclesiastical structures. It is a general rule that a treatment which is completely harmless is also very likely to be useless. It is an undertaking fraught with danger to commit oneself to the spiritual path. Thus quite a number of well-educated young people are seduced into joining sinister cults whose leaders work towards their own wealth at the cost of a progressive degradation of their enslaved disciples. They are all, in fact, contemporary manifestations of the Antichrist, whose qualities we have already considered. But he is to be found also as a highly ranking dignatory in the most respected denominations, at least during some periods of their history: indeed, the history of religion is a fearsome testimony of the power of truth to bring to the surface all inner corruption. This is, no doubt, one purpose of religious commitment. It may be the deeper work of the devil in the person of his earthly representative, the Antichrist. When the necessarily destructive role of evil in the development of human consciousness is accepted, we can live more at ease with it as part of the total cosmic situation. Only then can the transfiguring love of God flowing down to us be received in our soul. This is the beginning of a new dispensation whereby all that lives will be progressively loosed of its selfish proclivities and find supreme satisfaction in the present moment. "Sin is necessary . . .", as Julian of Norwich was indeed told.

There are two polarities of religious practice: fundamentalism on the one hand and an undisciplined savouring of all the world's great faiths on the other. Fundamentalism ranges from a scriptural literalism to an earnest intention of returning to the primary source of the tradition, the fundamentals of the belief structure. It provides the believer with an assurance that is of enormous help day by day, but it fails to do justice to the human mind in its forward thrust to new encounters and endeavours. Above all, it inhibits the work of the Holy Spirit in his constant revelation of new interpretations of abiding truths. As Jesus told his disciples, "It is for your good that I am leaving you. If I do not go, your Advocate will not come, whereas if I go, I will send him to you" (John 16:7). This is soon followed by the observation, "There is still much that I could say to you, but the burden would be too great now. However, when he comes who is the Spirit of truth, he will guide you into all the truth; for he will not speak on his own authority, but will tell you only what he hears; and he will make known to you the things that are coming. He will glorify me, for everything that he makes known to you he will draw from what is mine" (John 16:12–14). The Holy Spirit does not assume an autonomous function of enlightenment: he reveals the depth of the human soul to the individual as well as pointing to the future state, the advent of Christ himself in the universe. In this way we may start to be re-created in the divine image, so that we may then come to share in the very being of God. But before this far-off event can occur, nothing can remain hidden, unexamined, rejected or unassimilated. All must return to its Creator.

An undisciplined savouring of the various traditions of human inspiration as codified in their religious beliefs brings with it a liberating tolerance and a transcendence of dogmatic exclusiveness. But it also tends to obliterate the necessary boundaries that define an individual personality, so that the genius of the person is dissipated in vague generalities. A faith is of most use to the world when it is most true to its own insights. A meandering type of religion that borrows indiscriminately from divers sources in an attempt to please everyone soon dissolves into a benign message of universal goodwill that helps no one in particular. Heracleitus made the famous observation that one cannot find out the boundaries of the soul, so deep are they. And yet while we are alive we are bound in circumscribed personalities. The statement of Heracleitus casts light on the deep psychic contact between individuals, and between them and God through the mediation of the creatures of the intermediate dimension whom we have already considered: the angelic hierarchy and the communion of the departed, some of whom are indeed sanctified. In a somewhat similar way we are bound to a particular ego consciousness which in the end has to be transcended to a soul awareness with its apex of divine immanence. But we cannot yield the ego until it is well formed; then alone is it worthy of sacrifice to God. "A grain of wheat remains a solitary grain unless it falls into the ground and dies; but if it dies, it bears a rich harvest" (John 12:24). Jesus goes on to teach that the man who lives for himself alone is lost, but the one who expends himself freely in this world will be kept safe for eternal life. However, he must have something first to expend, hence the necessity for individual self-actualization.

It is evident that neither fundamentalism nor an hospitable welcoming of any new influence is enough, although both approaches have their strengths. The great world religions generally have at present a strong fundamentalist contingent. Its members are bellicose and naïvely assured of divine assistance because of the rectitude of their cause. War can then easily assume a holy character. The Zionist victory in Palestine precipitated the full force of Arab nationalism, which has been nourished by resurgent Islamic fundamentalism. When fundamentalist groups from opposing factions confront one another, no meaningful communication can take place. The same situation is true of dogmatic Marxism in confrontation with the broad sweep of western capitalism. It is only the threat of nuclear warfare that has preserved a semblance of peace in the greater counsels of the world. Where there has been regional warfare of a "conventional" type, as in Korea, Vietnam and the Middle East, the casualty figures have frequently been very large. And the tragedy is overwhelming. Nevertheless, the trend towards world peace, though still limited, is significant at the present time. The Russians have discountenanced the policies of Stalin, who is now regarded as a psychopathic personality by many of his countrymen. The slow tendency to liberalization seems to be gaining a certain momentum in the current climate of opinion, while the USSR and the USA are working out in agonizing detail a policy of progressive nuclear disarmament. But only when there is real trust among the leaders of the nations can general disarmament proceed in full measure. Bellicosity is the front that conceals a yawning chasm of weakness; reconciliation speaks of mutual strength.

For peace talks to start it is first necessary for both parties to acknowledge that unilateral victory is impossible. For these talks to proceed, a spirit of love has to warm the frigid souls of the negotiators, so that they cease to act as powerful politicians with hearts of stone and become frail human beings with hearts of flesh. What starts as an act of expediency gradually broadens through self-knowledge and humility to deep compassion. Then only do wars become inconceivable as the law of love informs and transfigures the moral law set out in the last five of the Ten Commandments. "Love cannot wrong a neighbour; therefore the whole law is summed up in love" (Romans 13:10). The problem is how to acquire that love, not as a temporary rapture, but as a constant inward presence. In fact it is given constantly by God's grace, but we have to be ready in our own lives to receive it. In the words of the Magnificat, "The hungry he has satisfied with good things, the rich sent empty away" (Luke 1:53). In the language of the Beatitudes, "How blest are those who know their need of God; the kingdom of Heaven is theirs" (Matthew 5:3). This poverty of spirit follows the long, arduous path of life when we are summarily disabused of all comforting illusions, when we enter the divine darkness and experience total separation from all human support as Jesus did during the period of his Passion. And then we know God as the coincidence of opposites, the resolution of all conflicting tendencies, the void that is the fullness of creation and yet stands outside it as an unknowable presence, fully available to all who call from the heart. "Come, all who are thirsty, come, fetch water; come, you who have no food, buy corn and eat; come and buy, not for money, not for a price" (Isaiah 55:1). With what then do we buy, since there is no price? Our gift is ourselves, while God's gift is himself. The enrichment is mutual as a new relationship is struck. "God became man in order that man might become God", says St Athanasius.

"He was made what we are that he might make us what he is himself", affirms St Irenaeus.

Is our present age any nearer to the transfiguration of man than were the long periods behind us, illuminated by the witness of the saints of antiquity? It is hard to make a firm judgement, but on the whole we do live in a healthier, more compassionate world than that of our forebears: ignorant, powerless and fearful. There were then bright sparks of saintliness in a sea of dark ignorance. The vastly improved social conditions in many countries with the correspondingly enhanced literacy of the masses has meant that the man in the street is now in contact with vast ranges of thought that were previously beyond his grasp. And so the Stygian darkness of earlier times has been lit up by a diffuse, pale glow of aspiring humanity. There seem to be fewer masters of the spiritual life, but a greater interest among the general run of people in the things of the mind and the spirit. The dominance of the media of mass communication has aided this dissemination of knowledge. Of course, this somewhat rosy assessment of human advancement is belied by vast areas of mass starvation and premature death brought about through the poor distribution of resources. Still, there is a wider awareness of these enormities in the greater world than in times past, with a corresponding eagerness to redress the balance of human resources to the benefit of the many who have nothing to call their own, not even basic food supplies. The present situation is murky as the young independent nations forcibly demonstrate their newly-found strength in their emancipated domains. It takes time for a young country to cope with the assimilation of its diverse elements, to say nothing of the urgency of economic progress and elementary education. The greater the weakness, the more necessary is the show of strength, whether of arms or cultural identity. It is in such an environment that religious fundamentalism is especially welcome, being emotionally satisfying as well as nationally affirming. It is good to have God on one's side, a god of judgement who favours his own disciples at the expense of heretics and unbelievers! Fundamentalist groups fan the flames of intolerance in many countries, working towards the eradication of anyone who threatens their domination. There is little love in the fundamentalist, only a fierce abhorrence that seeks to crush all opposing ideologies. He looks for an assurance that is, in fact, unattainable, not the love that alone can reconcile conflicting points of view in a synthesis that illuminates the individual genius to the benefit of the whole. Indeed, no gift flourishes in isolation; it has to be used and bestowed on the whole organism. We work to our best when we lose ourselves in forgetfulness in the joy of serving the community. Only then can an assurance of God's love come to us that fills us with renewed strength for the work ahead of us.

It is the general relaxation of moral principles, especially those pertaining to sex, that is one of the most conspicuous features of contemporary life. The situation is one of amorality, a total unconcern for moral standards, rather than vicious immorality, a deliberate flouting of those standards. Relationships are governed by emotional responses usually on a basis of urgent desire, but there is often little deeper commitment of the parties, so that marriage vows, when indeed they are made, are likely to be soon disregarded. One-parent families are increasingly common, while the practice of child abuse is emerging as a major social evil. It would be naïve to pretend that most of this is a novelty; whereas before it tended to be concealed beneath a façade of social respectability heavily impregnated by conventional religion, it has now been shown in its naked ugliness. For many people traditional values have been dismissed as archaic restraints heavily tinged with hypocrisy. The advent of seemingly safe sexual promiscuity following the development of successful contraceptive drugs has met with a dramatic check in the form of a previously unknown venereal disease, AIDS, which is as yet incurable. The virus of this terrible scourge apparently lay latent, possibly in Africa, until a mutation to virulence coincided with the worldwide sexual promiscuity and flaunting of unnatural practices of our own time. While I would not cite this as an example of God's wrath against a sinful generation – a God of love could not visit such suffering on his children – it seems evident to me that the law by which God sees to the government of the world is perfectly self-regulating. If it is desregarded, it hits back with effects often out of all proportion in suffering to the original disobedience that started the process. The account of the destruction of Sodom and Gomorrah is a quasi-historical application of this principle, as is also the probably more historical description of the drowning of Pharaoh's army in the Red Sea, and Joshua's complete annihilation of the cities of Jericho and Ai: the spiritually inadequate are supplanted by more worthy groups of people. Indeed, if these episodes are not seen in this context, the picture of God they portray is so terrifying that it would be difficult to trust in him, let alone love him. Fortunately, sins can be forgiven, hence the power of prayer by which means the Holy Spirit can infuse us with fresh resolve and inspiration to work towards the healing of the tragedy. In terms of the AIDS epidemic this inspiration embraces medical research aimed at immunization against as well as cure of the disease, social measures to prevent its spread as well as caring for its victims, and a fresh understanding of God's full purpose in the lives of his rational creatures. We were meant for a destiny higher than promiscuous genital satisfaction; only a knowledge of God himself can suffice in our lives, and then the appetites of the flesh will find their proper balance. It needs also to be remembered that some AIDS victims have acquired the disease adventitiously, following the therapeutic use of blood or its products that have been contaminated with the virus. Their lives may well have been models of chastity, but it is their burden to play their part in cleansing the world's stain. As we have already noted, none of us can evade responsibility for the corporate sin of our fellows, so inseparably are we all parts of the one body.

The progressive liberation of groups that had previously borne the stigma of discrimination, notably women, homosexuals, Jews, Blacks, and racial and religious minorities in general, has been accompanied by a release of resentment and anger on their part that has shown itself in an attitude of defiance towards the prevailing authorities and an aggressive desire for increasing power. This in turn not surprisingly evokes a reaction on the part of the established majority, who now feel threatened by the life styles and religious beliefs of those whom they previously despised if not actively persecuted. Indeed, as the basic law of physics has it: action and reaction are equal but opposite. For a time a liberal tolerance may accept the unfolding manifestation of new ways of living with sympathy, but once the process upsets the stability of the majority, they soon take steps to suppress all activity which could possibly end in chaos. Irresponsible liberalism can foster antinomianism, the flouting of the obligation to obey the moral law, whereas a rigid enforcement of traditional values ends up in such an imprisonment of the human spirit that all private endeavour is proscribed and inertia ensues. Both of these tendencies have been well represented in this century. The one thing they hold in common is a debased view of human nature; both are ultimately destructive of human endeavour as they undermine the power of the will to make independent decisions and then to implement them.

When the smouldering anger of various conflicting groups is ignited by personal affront, it can flare up with terrifying rapidity into communal violence. The world at present is in a similar state of incendiary instability. It is not surprising that we are constantly confronted with "the noise of battle near at hand and the news of battles far away", to quote Mark 13:7. The passage goes on to quieten our alarm, telling us that such things, and even worse, are bound to occur, for with them the birth-pangs of the new age begin. Adventism, the forecasting of the actual time of the appearance of Christ who brings in the new age, has been discountenanced by the Church, for on one level the advent is constantly being inaugurated, and on another we are preparing for it as we grow in spiritual awareness. At the time when the birth-pangs are most acute, all that has been fermenting deep within the psyche of the worldwide community rises to the surface with a shattering violence. But then it has to be accepted, accommodated, assimilated and given to God as our sacrifice. This is the dark part of our privilege in being created and in growing into maturity as people of integrity.

This may be the real harvest of our century of unrelieved violence. In its early years an exhilarating liberalism held sway, inspired by the evolutionary theories of Charles Darwin and Herbert Spencer. Then came the two world wars; their barely credible brutality shattered the belief in a virtually automatic progress based on education and economic security. In fact, of course, the belief was founded on a pathetic ignorance of human nature: the show of outer urbanity simply concealed a stinking cesspit of slowly fermenting vice and cruelty. Now, at last, the products of this subversive fermentation have been released into the general atmosphere, and the population recoils from the impact of its stench. But at least the corruption lies exposed, so that a more determined, enlightened, united effort can be made to cope with it. This is surely the way of personal, no less than communal, restoration of health.

Life, indeed, has been infused into the dry bones of generations apparently destroyed in the vicious wars of our time. A fresh generation, in fact generations, have come to maturity, and new styles of living have been explored in which money is not the over-all directive. We proceed precariously near the edge of a precipice of extinction, but the Spirit of

God has not left us. Our mistakes are the steps on the ladder of our proficiency. They may prove to be more authentic than the imposed dogmas of the various religious denominations, perhaps even illuminating those dogmas in a way that a professional ministry may fail to accomplish, at least until it too has come to terms with the darkness inside itself.

9

The Encompassing Light

Jean-Jacques Rousseau observed in *The Social Contract*, "Man is born free, and everywhere he is in chains". In the next century Karl Marx was to identify, at least to his own satisfaction, the origin of those chains in the prevailing economic system. Thus he ended his epoch-making *Communist Manifesto* with the clarion call, "The workers have nothing to lose in this revolution but their chains. They have a world to gain. Workers of the world, unite!" There is certainly much truth in Rousseau's observation and in Marx's diagnosis of the trouble. Where there are intolerable economic conditions the social order is little more than mindless slavery to the hard facts of poverty on the one hand and the unscrupulous employer on the other – if indeed employment is available.

Yet the affluent are also in chains. They are bound to their money and the demands their wealth places on them. There are also deeper chains than mere outer indigence, for we are all the products of our particular heredity and environment. These play a large part in determining how profitably we will use the benefits placed at our disposal. The implementation of social justice, as far as this has been possible in our own time, has certainly seen the end of the worst excesses of poverty and deprivation, but whether it has brought in its train any conspicuous happiness or true freedom in the lives and aspirations of the people is still an open question. While no one with intelligence would tolerate a return to the social conditions of the past, it is evident that the personal fulfilment lies in a realm far beyond mere affluence. At the most, material security provides a firm basis for human advancement, but it does not afford the individual the impetus for the work he has been educated to perform. We recall in this respect an observation made some 2,300 years ago:

> The man who loves money can never have enough, and the man who is in love with great wealth enjoys no return from it. This too is vanity. When riches multiply, so do those who live off them; and what advantage has the owner, except to look at them? Sweet is the sleep of the labourer whether he eats little or much; but the rich man owns too much and cannot sleep (Ecclesiastes 5:10–12).

The sweet content attributed to the labourer may seem a trifle idyllic, but the fine oracle of Zephaniah 3:11–13 amplifies the true spirit of poverty, "On that day, Jerusalem, you shall not be put to shame for your deeds by which you have rebelled against me; for then I will rid you of your proud and arrogant citizens, and never again shall you flaunt your pride on my holy hill. But I will leave in you a people afflicted and poor. The survivors in Israel shall find refuge in the name of the Lord; they shall no longer do wrong or speak lies, no words of deceit shall pass their lips; for they shall feed and lie down with no one to terrify them." It is these poor people who, in terms of the first Beatitude, have the kingdom of Heaven (Matthew 5:3). They are the poor in spirit, the ones who know their need of God. This poverty is acquired in the course of life when worldly riches are withdrawn and the love of God, the one thing necessary for eternal life, is revealed. It alone endures.

We are born with nothing outside ourselves, and so we leave the world as we proceed to the unknown, yet dimly remembered, realms that lie ahead of us. As we have conducted ourselves here, so will the realm be that awaits us and the souls with whom we can communicate most easily. While we are alive on the earth, we have to encounter much darkness as part of the greater unfolding of our personality, but the end of all this suffering is our identification with the inner lives of our fellow creatures. Our experience of the polarities of darkness and light, of evil and good, is a part of the pageant of universal growth. If there were no temptation of evil, there would be no awareness of goodness. In a society where hatred was not countenanced there would be little love (of the type that will sacrifice itself), but only a safe, detached benevolence that effected no relationship with anything. Out of the terrible events of our tortured century much potential good has emerged. I refer to the liberation of previously subject groups of people. But the exuberance of their newly-found strength has provoked a corresponding reaction on the part of the more staid, conservative elements of the population. This too is a necessary part of progress, lest one particular trend should overwhelm the world. Caution and discernment are less attractive counsels than is an enthusiastic exploration of uncharted realms of experience, but all have to work in reverent obedience to the law whereby God governs his universe. The end of life is not so much sectarian triumph as loving reconciliation, not so much the exclusion of evil as the total transfiguration of all the creation into the eternal light of God, as the physical body of Jesus was transfigured, and later resurrected, into the glory of the Godhead.

I sometimes think about Arthur Koestler, a representative man of the twentieth century, whose novel *Darkness at Noon* formed the basis of a previous chapter of this book. Born in Central Europe of Jewish parents, he exhibited the intelligence, zest for living, and adventurous spirit so typical of the ancient people of God. He was successively a Zionist – until he was disillusioned by the situation in British-administered Palestine – a Communist fighting in the bloody Spanish civil war of the thirties, and then a captive in the hands of the nationalist forces under Franco. During his imprisonment he had a remarkable mystical experience that changed the course of his life. He was too honest and intelligent a man to confuse spirituality with organized religion – and certainly none of the current religious denominations, whether eastern or western, could inspire a discerning seeker with great enthusiasm, although esoteric offshoots might stimulate the appetite for a limited period. His interest moved latterly in the direction of psychical research, and in his will he endowed a chair for that nebulous, and scientifically unpopular, subject. Several universities distanced themselves from the bequest, and it is to the credit of the University of Edinburgh that the money was accepted and a department set up. Time will tell whether its researches can establish psychical phenomena categorically within a scientific framework. The Koestlers, husband and wife, took their lives together when they knew they were suffering from progressive, ultimately fatal, illnesses. Here we see an adventurous life of exuberant activity moving dramatically to the spiritual dimension, but then stasis, increasing debilitation and the sad resignation of suicide. One is tempted to speculate what the outcome might have been had he and his wife submitted to the discipline of a particular spiritual path as defined in one of the world's great religious traditions. While on earth, no matter how enlightened we may have become, we have to enter fully into the existence of the many less aware people around us. This is the meaning of incarnation on a personal level, and it finds its supreme example in the life of Jesus, the Word made flesh. He did not spurn his mother's womb or the embarrassing process of infancy, childhood, adolescence and early manhood, before the brief period of active ministry formed the peak of his life and crucifixion its end. Humility is indeed the basic spiritual virtue.

It is therefore worth while plumbing the depths of humility to see its place in the spiritual life. It comes to us when we do not know how to proceed, when all previous teachings and certainties have been found to be unavailing. When we are in the suffocating darkness of our own hell, like that of Job or the Prodigal Son, we are suddenly confronted by a light of radiance that illuminates our total situation. We at once accept its glow and loving warmth with relief, but as it leads us on to the fuller light, it makes demands on us. It requires nothing less than a complete change in heart, so that we may take up the darkness of the world around us in the light that had so recently lightened our own darkness. As we proceed into the full strength of the light, so we have, at the same time, to penetrate the full darkness of life and accept its corroding stench: the higher the ascent, the deeper the descent. Nothing human, indeed nothing created, no matter how debased or depraved it may appear, can any longer be alien to us. And as we assume the world's darkness in our ascent to the Supreme Light whom we call God, so that darkness is lightened and its obscurity is made visible and intelligible. The light not only encompasses us in a radiant aura but also purifies the depth of our personality until we may be an immaculate chalice of God's uncreated light. As our depths are illuminated, so we take our place in the light of God. It is then that we know the meaning of love. It had, of course, not been far from our awareness since the time of our release, but at last it becomes integrated into our very being. And then it radiates to the entire cosmos as a beam of the love of God. The light of God in this way releases the love that is native to the soul but usually imprisoned in it.

In that love everything is taken up, the unclean as well as the clean, the evil as well as the good, the darkness and the light, the resentment and the pardon, and all are transfigured into the supreme love of God and the uncreated light of his outflowing energies, indeed of his very essence as far as we may dare speak of these summits of reality. Of God's love and light our own corresponding qualities are at most pale reflections. But they may increase in strength.

The process is slow and painful, for the will of the sluggish, unyielding creature strives constantly against the divine law of growth and reconciliation, until its ignorance is dispelled by the light of purification. No creature is outside this transfiguring presence.

We thought much earlier on about the pot that God had created misshapen, the person so defective in mind through congenital abnormality as to be a mere parody of human nature. We also reflected on the tragedy of a once vibrant personality now shut off from the world because of senile dementia. But now we can begin to see, by virtue of enhanced spiritual understanding, that all is well in God's greater counsels. What we now are is what we have to give to the world. Behind the tragic mask of total impotence and humiliation there lies a soul gaining in experience for work that lies ahead of it in a realm beyond mortal limitations of time and space. In any situation of tragedy the question is the same: what does God want me to do with it? If it cannot be ameliorated by rational means, the truth still shines out: the greater the humiliation, the greater the mastery; the greater the suffering, the greater the glory. The passion of Christ has to be repeated in the lives of all rational creatures. Its end is universal resurrection. And then the light is of a quality that transfigures the lesser light as well as the darkness of our mortal lives and the world in which we move day by day. All this development calls for a progressive unfolding of the soul in the reaches of the life beyond mortal death; as it comes to know Christ better, so the soul partakes more fully of the Christian way of loving service, sacrifice, and rebirth into the glory of the risen Lord.

God has boldly been defined as transcending all the qualities of the mind, even those of good and evil. In him there is the supreme good whose created image, the Lord Jesus, is love. To learn this love, not merely intellectually but also in experience, is the object of all life. The instruments on the way are the full complement of individual attributes; the lights on the path are truth, beauty and goodness. It takes so long to master this work of love, which is accompanied by a downpouring of healing light, that time dissolves into eternity and the present moment is the constant point of action.

Fount Paperbacks

Fount is one of the leading paperback publishers of religious books and below are some of its recent titles.

- ☐ **THROUGH SEASONS OF THE HEART**
  John Powell   £4.95
- ☐ **WORDS OF LIFE FROM JOHN THE BELOVED**
  Frances Hogan   £2.95
- ☐ **MEISTER ECKHART** Ursula Fleming   £2.95
- ☐ **CHASING THE WILD GOOSE** Ron Ferguson   £2.95
- ☐ **A GOOD HARVEST** Rita Snowden   £2.50
- ☐ **UNFINISHED ENCOUNTER** Bob Whyte   £5.95
- ☐ **FIRST STEPS IN PRAYER** Jean-Marie Lustiger   £2.95
- ☐ **IF THIS IS TREASON** Allan Boesak   £2.95
- ☐ **RECLAIMING THE CHURCH** Robin Greenwood   £2.95
- ☐ **GOD WITHIN US** John Wijngaards   £2.95
- ☐ **GOD'S WORLD** Trevor Huddleston   £2.95
- ☐ **A CALL TO WITNESS** Oliver McTernan   £2.95
- ☐ **GOODNIGHT LORD** Georgette Butcher   £2.95
- ☐ **FOR GOD'S SAKE** Donald Reeves   £3.50
- ☐ **GROWING OLDER** Una Kroll   £2.95
- ☐ **THROUGH THE YEAR WITH FRANCIS OF ASSISI**
  Murray Bodo   £2.95

All Fount Paperbacks are available at your bookshop or newsagent, or they can be ordered by post from Fount Paperbacks, Cash Sales Department, G.P.O. Box 29, Douglas, Isle of Man. Please send purchase price plus 22p per book, maximum postage £3. Customers outside the UK send purchase price, plus 22p per book. Cheque, postal order or money order. No currency.

NAME (Block letters) _____

ADDRESS_____

_____

_____